Empowering the Connected Physician in the E-Patient Era

The constantly evolving digital world must be used in the practice of medicine to improve the care of patients. However, the only way to do so effectively is via evidence-based, meaningful and strategic use. *Empowering the Connected Physician in the E-Patient Era* provides practical guidance in this mission and is thus essential reading for all health stakeholders looking into approaching this.

Drawing on the author's research and consulting practice, as well as on the practical experience of managers in medium-large organizations worldwide, the book will provide a proven framework to improve the development and implementation of physicians' empowering digital programs in these organizations, a step-by-step guide for how companies can develop and implement programs aiming at empowering physicians while empowering patients. It is an engaging how-to/how-not-to book which will include tips, advice and critical reviews that every stakeholder must have in order to participate in the evolving healthcare system and be more active in making strategic patient-centered choices.

This book will help healthcare organizations chart a course within this new territory and thereby improve their ability to engage with empowered patients.

Letizia Affinito is the Founder and CEO of Brandnew MC and has worked for over 25 years in Strategic Marketing Communications Management both as manager and consultant. She has advised several multinational companies and organizations on online/offline communication strategy matters. Author of the international book *Socialize Your Patient Engagement Strategy* and *e-patient e social media* published in Italy, Letizia has a Ph.D. in Management and teaches as Adjunct Professor at Boston College, The James A. Woods, S.J., College of Advancing Studies, and Saint John's University of Rome. Her education includes the Teaching with Cases Online, the Case Method Teaching Seminar (Parts I and II), the Executive Program in Digital Marketing at Harvard Business School, and the Young Managers Executive Programme at INSEAD.

Empowering the Connected Physician in the E-Patient Era

How Physicians' Empowerment on Digital Health Tools Can Improve Patient Empowerment and Boost Health(care) Outcomes

LETIZIA AFFINITO

Routledge
Taylor & Francis Group

LONDON AND NEW YORK

First published 2019
by Routledge
2 Park Square, Milton Park, Abingdon, Oxon OX14 4RN

and by Routledge
711 Third Avenue, New York, NY 10017

Routledge is an imprint of the Taylor & Francis Group, an informa business

© 2019 Letizia Affinito

British Library Cataloguing-in-Publication Data
A catalogue record for this book is available from the British Library

Library of Congress Cataloging-in-Publication Data
A catalog record has been requested for this book

ISBN: 978-1-138-49737-5 (hbk)
ISBN: 978-1-351-01890-6 (ebk)

To those of you genuinely committed to doing good while doing well.

Letizia Affinito

Contents

Figures

Tables

Acknowledgements

Saying this book is "by Letizia Affinito" is overstated. Without the significant contributions made by other people, this book would certainly not exist.

At the top of the list is everyone who, without even knowing me, accepted to contribute with his/her content and accompanied me on this exciting journey. Having worked in the healthcare field for a long time, I have been following a number of "gurus" dedicated to a number of topics covered in this book. Indeed, I've never met many of them before. It's been a joy and a blessing to receive their trust and support.

I knew, from the very beginning, how demanding the topic was and the difficulties I could have encountered but I got to the end. I was truly blessed to have a number of extraordinary journey companions trusting me and dedicated to the project. I am indebted to each of them.

I would like to give a special thanks to a number of executives from many different health organizations who were willing to share their case histories: David J. Cook, M.D., Chief Clinical and Operating Officer, Jiahui Health, Shanghai Peoples Republic of China; Jennifer Dearborn, Director, public affairs at Concord Hospital; C. Martin Harris, MD, MBA, Associate Vice President of the Health Enterprise & Chief Business Officer at Dell Medical School; Sharon K. Prinsen, registered nurse and a nurse administrator at Mayo Clinic, for patiently reviewing my contents and giving their insights and comments.

I owe a lot to Sara Berg, senior communications specialist at the American Medical Association; Kamal Jethwani, MD MPH, Senior Director, Connected Health Innovation at Partners HealthCare; Michalis A. Michael, CEO at DigitalMR; Devin Peek, Senior Communication Designer at IDEO; PwC; and Usertesting for sharing their contents and charts.

A big thank you to *FADOI - Scientific Society of Internal Medicine* for its trust and support on the Web in Salute independent research project which has provided me with the most recent insights to include in this book.

I would like to make a special note of Amy Laurens as my publisher at Taylor & Francis who has enthusiastically supported this book from the moment she received the proposal, and of Alex Atkinson, Editorial Assistant, for her precious support and commitment.

Preface

My first approach to health marketing management dates back to 1993 while taking my CSS Program at Harvard. At that time a "new" trend was starting in the health industry: communicating to the patient!

More than 20 years have passed by and I am witnessing a "new" trend in the health industry: the rise of the empowered patient!

"Patient Empowerment" is becoming more and more important for successful health organizations and healthcare outcomes. Nevertheless, we can still count on a single hand the few organizations which have been able to successfully pursue it so far.

The issue is that pharma/biotech companies and healthcare organizations have focused on empowering the patient, mostly chronic patients, with standalone initiatives, under-estimating the central role of the physician.

Indeed, physicians and patients are part of an articulated system which everybody willing to commit to patient empowerment should consider in its whole. In addition, too often we hear about new technologies for the physicians, patients, and healthcare organizations. More than investing and spending on the latest futuristic technologies, we should focus on implementing and managing effectively the digital technologies already available in our organizations.

After researching for more than nine years, I decided to conclude the "journey" started in 2015 with *Socialize Your Patient Engagement Strategy*,1 with a book focused on how to develop and implement a physician empowering digital strategy to provide health managers with the best practices, approaches and tools to create value for patients, physicians, and healthcare organizations.

While access to information has improved, health managers have little time to review, select, and read all the materials providing insights and tools on this important topic. This book is an effort to scout, select and curate the best insights and ideas which have been published on the topic, integrating them into a comprehensive framework.

From new technology adoption, to human-centered design and the best tools for both physician and patient empowerment (including augmented reality), *Empowering the Connected Physician in the E-Patient Era* is currently the first book specifically designed to meet healthcare professionals learning needs.

I view this book as a starting point of a constructive exchange of ideas for further learning that hopefully will help make patient empowerment digital strategy a consolidated practice. I hope you will find value in these pages and will enjoy reading it as much as I did writing it.

Letizia Affinito
laffinito@brandnewmc.com
Rome, Italy

Note

1 Letizia Affinito and John Mark (2015), *Socialize Your Patient Engagement Strategy: How Social Media and Mobile Apps Can Boost Health Outcomes*. Abingdon: Routledge.

Introduction

Health system executives, policymakers, purchasers and payers all play an important role in solving worldwide healthcare cost crisis. Indeed we all must know by now that they will not succeed unless physicians buy in their mission and commit to it as their own.

Talking about patient empowerment, it is generally accepted that it is the holy grail of health promotion and that it presents a number of advantages for physicians, payers, health systems and the patients themselves.

The term "Patient Empowerment" is, indeed, a concept increasingly used to describe situations where patients are encouraged to proactively manage their own health. It is more and more considered as critical to increase the quality of healthcare, but "how Patient Empowerment will be successfully achieved?" Apart from psychological connotations, patient empowerment in everyday practice depends on digital tools and how they are used.

One question is often raised by healthcare managers and/or HCPs: Is digital health technology effectively empowering patients?

Many times in the past few years, I have been asking "How can physicians empower their patients if they themselves are not being effectively empowered by their organizations or other stakeholders?" These are just some of the key questions I try to answer in this book.

In fact, regardless of the extraordinary advances in medications and technology, healthcare systematically falls short when it is expected to reliably meet its consumers' needs (i.e. physicians and patients). In a situation where you have to deal with constantly increasing complexity, the tough work and commitment of individual physicians are not enough any more to assure valuable, high-quality care. Healthcare will need to move to a team-based patient-centered approach where doctors must be key players in the digital era transformation.

Indeed, conquering physicians' support takes more than plain incentives. Leaders at all levels must rely on a great deal of positivism, audacity and flexibility.

To help healthcare leaders engage physicians in the pursuit of their organizations' greater goals, Thomas H. Lee et al. (2014) suggest a framework (chapter 10), based on the writings of the economist and sociologist Max Weber, who described four motivations that drive social action (that is, action in response to others' behavior). Adapted for healthcare professionals, these are shared purpose, self-interest, respect and tradition. Leaders can use these levers to earn doctors' buy-in and bring about the change the system so urgently needs.

The organizations committed to improving efficiency, deliver the best outcomes, increase their market share and retain as long as recruit the best people, will be the ones that can help physicians to live up to their aspirations as caregivers—to understand that giving up their autonomy is not actually submission but a noble act of humility in the interest of their patients.[1]

We all deserve an opportunity to be in good health. Physicians' role is, of course, to help patients. Sadly, we often see patients' frustrations with the healthcare system itself directed toward physicians who, at the same time are under increasing pressures on a number of fronts. Making physicians the primary target of patient anger will not solve problems we all face as humans who will, at some point, need healthcare. Patients need doctors. Doctors need patients. We need to find a way to value both.

As stated by the World Health Organization, health is more than not being ill but rather "a state of complete physical, mental and social well-being and not merely the absence of disease or infirmity."

Only if empowered patients can achieve the health they deserve. The "e" in e-patient can mean many things, but if health is a basic human right, then empowerment is the only "e" ensuring that right.

Being empowered means being able to meet certain fundamental needs (i.e. time, engagement in shared decision-making, knowledge-skills-values, self-esteem, caregivers, medical professionals, friends), which healthcare managers need to put in place before they can make accurate, informed decisions about health.

Doctors also have a hierarchy of needs (i.e. right tools, team coordination, safe work environment, competence, skill development, education and training resources, integrity, diligence, empathy, intelligence, civility, flexibility, mental and physical health).

They need to be healthy first—just like patients. Then, they need the right personal characteristics, training and support to be better able to do their job—helping patients.

Empowering patients and doctors assures they can work together. They both have a lot to bring to the table. Empowered patients are better able to collaborate. Empowered doctors are more able to adapt to patients' needs and communicate well to build trust. They need each other. If they support each other, the entire healthcare system will benefit.

As we'll see, practical approaches to empower patients vary in scope, aim and technology.

Health literacy of patients, remote access to health services, and self-care mechanisms are the most valued ways to accomplish Patient Empowerment. Current technology already allows establishing the first steps in the road ahead, but a change of attitude by all stakeholders (i.e. professionals, patients, policy makers, etc.) is required.

A Digital Health Strategy designed around physicians and aiming at reaching effective patient empowerment can play a major role in driving the needed transformation. Being user-centered is the strategy that will support the business in the long term.

While there are books that focus on specific healthcare managers and stakeholders within different types of organizations, in this book I recognize that effective patient empowerment crosses all organizational boundaries. That is, putting patient empowerment first is a priority for ALL healthcare professionals and this book focuses on how to achieve that and provide better value for organizations (in terms of healthcare outcomes) and patients (in terms of better service and improved health).

The healthcare industry has a unique opportunity to use Internet and digital tools to provide better value for both organizations (in terms of healthcare outcomes) and for patients (in terms of better service and improved health). By reading this book, you are taking a step forward to seize that opportunity.

What you will learn from this book

The constantly evolving digital world must be used in the practice of medicine to improve the care of patients. However, the only way to do so effectively is via evidence-based, meaningful and strategic use. *Empowering the Connected*

Physician in the E-Patient Era provides practical guidance in this mission and is thus essential reading for all health stakeholders looking into approaching this.

Drawing on the author's research and consulting practice, as well as on the practical experience of managers in medium-large organizations worldwide, the book will provide a proven framework to improve the development and implementation of physicians' empowering digital programs in these organizations, a step-by-step guide for how companies can develop and implement programs aiming at empowering physicians while empowering patients. It is an engaging how-to/how-not-to book which will include tips, advice, and critical reviews that every stakeholder must have in order to participate in the evolving healthcare system and be more active in making strategic patient-centered choices.

This book will help healthcare organizations chart a course within this new territory and thereby improve their ability to engage with empowered patients.

Dr. Ferguson's vision was of a truly transformed role for consumers in their healthcare. There are many ways in which consumer scholars can contribute to this transformation. I focus on three key themes that I believe will help lead us to a future in which:

1. people take responsibility for their own health;
2. people understand their health choices;
3. people address the challenges of maintaining healthy behaviors over the long term.

In particular, the book will highlight four priority areas for actions (or levers):

1. *Improving health literacy (e.g. websites; targeted mass digital campaigns).* The starting point to transform the digital tools as a useful technology for patient and physician self-empowerment in healthcare is the ability to unleash the health literacy-driven power of the patient. Companies that push the responsibility for doing this to the widest and lowest possible levels in the organization will be the successful ones.
2. *Improving self-care (e.g. self-management education; self-monitoring; self-treatment).* Behind the democratic view of a patient-centered health system lies a significant focus and investment in self-management education, self-monitoring and self-treatment tools and training. Indeed, companies can re-ignite and nurture the patients' self-care abilities by developing valuable tools and delivering tailor-made training programs.
3. *Improving patient safety (e.g. adherence to treatment regimens; equipping patients for safer self-care).* The role patients can play in improving the safety of their care has been recognized only recently, and research into this issue is still in its early stages. Nevertheless, successful partnerships with patients to reduce errors and improve safety can only occur in environments where

patient involvement is valued and supported. Issues of health literacy must also be tackled before information about safety and risk can be effectively communicated to patients and acted upon by them.

To help companies realize the goal of successfully developing and implementing a physician empowering strategy, the book will show how to effectively leverage health digital tools to help organizations build a patient-centric health management strategy. Each chapter will include illustrative case studies from a range of organizations and/or physicians around the globe.

The book will conclude with a key message: true change is unlikely to occur in the absence of a holistic action plan and its effective execution. In support of this, the book will provide guidance on how to set up such a plan to successfully architect, develop and execute a widespread physician empowerment strategy from within the organization.

What you will find in this book

I have structured the book into three parts. The first part presents an overview of the current situation and the main basic concepts and definitions you need to learn before embarking on an empowering digital health program. The second provides some useful tools to design and implement a successful empowering digital strategy, The third and final part provides an overview of the actions and tools to help physicians empower their patients. These three parts comprise nine chapters.

Part I: Defining patient empowerment in the digital era and the physicians' empowerment process

Chapter 1: Patient empowerment as a process: Creating and capturing value

This chapter introduces you to the basic concepts of patient empowerment and both online and offline actions/tools to better empower patients. We start from the question: What is patient empowerment? What is the role of physicians in patient empowerment? Which are the main barriers to physician's empowerment? Next we discuss the main steps in the physician and patient empowerment process—from understanding physician's needs to designing patient-driven health digital strategies and integrated management programs, to building patient relationships and capturing value for the organization and/or the healthcare system. Finally, we discuss the major trends and forces affecting healthcare management in this age of digital technologies and patient engagement.

Chapter 2: Physicians' reluctance to engage with technology

Most companies do not succeed in their efforts to new technologies adoption because they merely import their digital tools in the healthcare setting and in physicians hands. In this chapter we are going to explore what is the primary advantage of a patient–physician digital strategy over a purely digital one and how developing a successful strategy can help organizations form and strengthen relationships with both physicians and patients in ways that also benefit the organization.

Part II: Developing a clear and sustainable digital strategy

Chapter 3: A simple model of the Digital Health Strategy Process

Having a shared strategy can highly contribute to successful physician and patient empowerment with digital tools. In this chapter we will introduce a seven-step digital health strategy model aiming at creating value for physicians, patients and healthcare systems. In the first six steps, healthcare organizations act to understand physicians, create physicians value and build strong physician relationships and collaborations. In the final step, organizations bring back the rewards of creating superior value. In fact, by creating value for physicians, they consequently capture value from them in the form of patient empowerment, healthcare outcomes, and patient QOL. We'll also see how to make it a shared process for physician's empowerment. I'll present each step individually.

Chapter 4: Listening to physicians: How behavioral analytics and social media fuel more personalized communication (online market research and web listening)

In the first step of the Digital Health Strategy Process Model, healthcare organizations work to understand physicians and patient needs, wants, and limitations. The Internet offers the opportunity to do this and also engage with physicians and patients' communities. Listening and engaging must be an iterative process which never stops. This is how you build great customer experiences.

In this chapter we will explore the definitions of passive and active listening and see how passive listening can be far more action-oriented and intent-filled than it sounds. Both types of listening can lead to a lot of action; after all, isn't that the point of listening? We'll present the type of analysis you need for leverage and possible applications for both passive and active listening. Finally, we will explore how managers gain insights into patients' needs and how companies develop and manage information about important health system elements: physicians, patients, competitors, products and other relevant stakeholders.

Chapter 5: Developing a data strategy to gain physician insights for better decision making

In this chapter we will explore how managers gain insights into physicians/patients' needs and the health system. We look at how organizations develop and manage data about important health system elements: physicians, patients, competitors, products and communication programs. To succeed in today's health system organizations must know how to turn mountains of information into fresh customer insights that will help them deliver greater value to customers.

Chapter 6: How to ignite adoption and diffusion of new digital tools

Adoption and diffusion are probably more important than new product development aspects of technological innovation because that's where the "donkey falls"—so to speak—and any innovation that doesn't plan for adoption and diffusion is on the right road to failure even if the technology itself is outstanding. In this chapter, after introducing the innovation process, we will explore the methods/tools to build successful adoption and diffusion among both physicians and consumers/patients. Finally we will analyze what are the expected digital health benefits and how to design and introduce evidence-based tools.

Chapter 7: Opinion leader influencer mapping and management

The number of factors influencing physician-prescribing decisions and his/her communication with patients continues to grow, including clinical experience, journal articles, CME activity, managed care, detailing, events, journal advertising, patient requests, online information seeking, etc. However, one of the most impactful influences on physicians has remained consistent: national, regional and/or local key opinion leaders (KOL). In this chapter we will explore how to accurately identify online/offline key opinion leaders to successfully promote digital health tools, initiatives and projects aiming at empowering patients. We'll see how the network effect and the diffusion theory play a critical role in making opinion leaders mapping and management very important.

Part III: Actions and tools to help physicians empower their patients

Chapter 8: Patient empowerment: A process and an outcome

Empowerment-based interventions include both a process and an outcome component. The process component occurs when the true purpose of the intervention is to increase the patient's capacity to think critically and make autonomous, informed decisions. The outcome component occurs when there is a measurable increase in the patient's ability to make autonomous, informed decisions. In this chapter we are going to explore both traditional and digital methods and tools physicians can use to inform, engage, involve and empower patients.

Chapter 9: Creating the right setting to promote physicians, empowerment

From the mindset of health care professionals to the lack of an internal protocol, training, and data security, barriers to the adoption of health digital tools abound. In this chapter we'll explore successful approaches to develop and implement an empowering internal healthcare environment.

Note

1 Thomas H. Lee, MD, and Toby Cosgrove, MD (2014), "Engaging doctors in the health care revolution." *Harvard Business Review*.

Part I

Defining patient empowerment in the digital era and the physicians' empowerment process

Patient empowerment as a process

1

Creating and capturing value

Societal and technological developments are creating an increasing pressure to move toward more extensive patient empowerment. As part of that process, governments are expected to provide reliable digital personalized health and well-being information. Such information is essential for effective self-management and health improvement by citizens.

In the last few years, much time and attention have been devoted to "empowering" patients, and from the patients' viewpoint, to learning how to become an empowered patient. But what does an empowered patient mean? I keep witnessing a certain degree of confusion in this regard. Indeed, if on one hand developing an effective patient-empowering digital strategy is one of the biggest challenges in today's evolving healthcare industry, on the other hand starting off on the right foot requires having a clear understanding and agreement on some basic concepts at the basis of a successful digital strategy capable to create and capture patient value.

In this chapter we introduce the basic concepts of patient empowerment. We start by defining patient empowerment and then discuss the role of physicians and the importance of their empowerment for a better and valuable patient empowerment. Finally we'll see which are the main barriers to physicians' empowerment.

We'll begin our journey with a **leading case history** on patient empowerment in action at Mayo Clinic, ranked in the U.S. News & World Report rankings of top hospitals as the #1 hospital overall, as well as #1 in more specialties than any other hospital in the nation. The secret to Mayo Clinic's success is its commitment to the patient centrality guiding principle.

In 2014, motivated by a strong willingness to provide their patients with well-defined and communicated care expectations, David J. Cook and his team at the Mayo Clinic developed and implemented a standardized practice model over a three-year period (2010–2012) that significantly reduced variation and improved predictability of care in adult cardiac surgery.[1]

The result was, among others, the development of the interactive Mayo myCare program, which used an iPad to provide patients with detailed descriptions of their treatment plans and clinical milestones, educational materials, a daily "To Do" list, and to report their progress and identify problems to their providers.

The first step was to analyze the cost elements in the operating rooms, intensive care units, and on the patient floor. They found that unwarranted variation in the care process negatively affected the value of care (outcomes divided by cost).

As a second step, before focusing on a solution they delineated and defined all the steps of the optimal care model for routine cardiac surgery that comprised determining both best practices and ways that patients could become more effective partners in their own recovery.

Based on the results of the previous step, to empower patients and establish their expectations, they committed to effectively providing the following to them:

- Plan of Stay which included a "Plan of Day" outlining expected daily clinical milestones and providing a daily patient "To Do" list which was linked to their clinical status and the recovery events (Figure 1.1).
- Modular Educational materials about their surgery, their medical conditions, and expected care events each day in the hospital.
- Gaining Strength Modules which established daily expectations for physical activities such as walking and breathing exercises and provided patients with tools to self-assess and report things like pain and mobility.
- Recovery-Planning information on how patients should care for themselves after discharge.

An iPad was selected as an ideal means to convey this information to patients and have them report their progress and problems to providers.

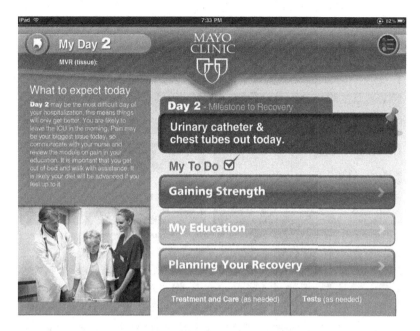

Figure 1.1 A screenshot of Day 2 of a typical plan of day
Source: Mayo Clinic.

Much care was dedicated also to the implementation stage starting from the accurate and clear definition of the participants, to the entire new care process with the launch of the Mayo myCare program in February 2012.

Then they designed the following care process:

1. Prior to surgery patients were provided with an iPad and trained for 30 minutes in using the program by a registered nurse.
2. A registered nurse then followed up with patients daily during their hospital stay to answer any questions they might have and make sure they understood how to use the program.

Most importantly, they accurately measured the program's outcomes as follows:

1. After the first 30 days of patient use, they evaluated patterns of program and content utilization by day, content type and content format.
2. They then modified the program to better meet patients' needs.

Before and after surgery, patients used the iPad to learn about the plan of day, work through their "To Do" list, and complete their daily education,

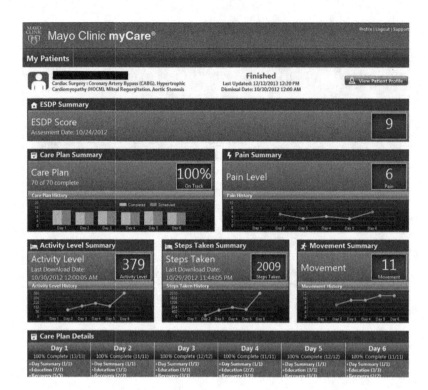

Figure 1.2 Screenshot of the patient dashboard including a predictor for the need for discharge support, compliance with the care plan, daily self-assessment of pain and mobility, and completion of education and recovery-planning modules. "ESDP" means Early Screen for Discharge Planning, a tool that predicts a patient's need for support after he or she is discharged

Source: Mayo Clinic.

self-assessments, and recovery-planning modules. The data was aggregated on a server in the cloud and configured into dashboards that the nurses and physicians caring for the patients could view (Figure 1.2).

A population and individual patient dashboard showed all patients on the care plan and provided alerts when patients were deviating from their plans. The providers could also click on an individual patient's name to view a dashboard for him or her.

The program triggered provider interventions when 1) a patient's self-assessment tool predicted patients might require home healthcare or skilled-nursing services at discharge, 2) patients were not completing their daily education or recovery-planning modules, and 3) a patient's self-reported mobility was too low or pain scores were too high.

Following discharge, patients were surveyed about their satisfaction with their hospitalization and surgical experience as well as their comfort in using the myCare program.

While the program was innovative and successful, the Mayo project faced a common challenge in healthcare IT projects; developed as a standalone program it could not be integrated into a major EMR transition and the program was eclipsed.

Defining patient empowerment

Probably one of the first and main issues when dealing with patient empowerment is the multiple ways in which it is defined not only depending on the context and objectives but also on the culture, mindset and background of each stakeholder.

To get started, let's clarify the issue of "power." Some authors claim that empowerment has nothing to do with power, thus nothing to do with giving or taking power (Anderson and Fannell 2010)[2]. On the other hand, others like Laverack (2005)[3] or Peña and Gil (2007)[4] think that power is at the core of the concept of empowerment. As pointed out by Page and Czuba (1999)[5] empowerment is not possible if power is inherent in positions or people. Thus it is fundamental to expect its shift from one person or group to another. It is also crucial to note that power is not only having the necessary knowledge, but also being able to exercise a choice based on that knowledge (Laverack 2005)[6]. If a given knowledge is not applicable, the person may feel even more powerless.

I strongly believe that empowerment has nothing to do with power and much more to do with responsibility, trust and sense of control over a disease.

In addition, it is interesting to note that if on one hand "empowerment" has always been defined as an emancipation process in which a disadvantaged person is empowered to exercise his/her rights and participate actively in society, the notion of "patient empowerment" has, on the other hand, always been used to refer to patients at large to emphasize their evolving role. Let us, therefore, take a closer look at the notion of patient empowerment as evidenced in the scientific literature.

Patient empowerment is generally used to refer to patients' control over their health and their condition, as well as their ability to be more involved in their healthcare. In other words, patient empowerment enables patients to "manage their healthcare and advocate for themselves as they use healthcare services" (Helmer et al. 2011).[7]

Gibson, in a review about Patient Empowerment in health, redefined empowerment as a process of helping people to assert control over the factors which affect their health.[8]

Another literature review defines Patient Empowerment as a continuous process through which patients (and patient groups) work in partnership with their healthcare system. The objective of this collaboration is to enable patients to become more responsible for and involved in their treatment and health care.

For the aim of this book we'll refer to the definition provided by the WHO which defines empowerment as "a *process* through which people gain greater control over decisions and actions affecting their health" and should be seen as both an individual and a community process.[9]

Four components have been reported as being fundamental to the process of patient empowerment: 1) understanding by the patient of his/her role; 2) acquisition by patients of sufficient knowledge to be able to engage with their healthcare provider; 3) patient skills; and 4) the presence of a facilitating environment. Based on these four components, empowerment can be defined as:

> A process in which patients understand their role, are given the knowledge and skills by their healthcare provider to perform a task in an environment that recognizes community and cultural differences and encourages patient participation.[10]

The best way to define patient empowerment would be to define it as an embracing practice that motivates patients to be mindfully involved in their providers' care services. The final goal of empowering patients is to guide them in the development of self-awareness and self-care while promoting patients as equal partners in their healthcare decisions.

In the face of different definitions, the shared core idea about patient empowerment depicts it as an attempt for patients to take charge of their own health.

Empowering patients with digital technologies

Nowadays, beyond cognitive connotations, technology and the way it is used is central in the empowerment of patients, mostly when they are affected by a chronic disease.[11]

Based on a literature review of 266 papers in 2013, Jorge Calvillo et al. highlight that there is a wide spectrum of technologies empowering patients. There are initiatives that use promising technologies (such as games and virtual worlds or textile monitoring), and others reuse traditional technologies (e.g. audio call or video recording).

Web services and communication networks have been reported as being the most used technologies (74 and 51 articles, respectively) to make remote communication and access to health information and services easier.

Aside from them, both Personal Health Records (PHR) and Electronic Health Record (EHR) approaches share superior positions. Very similar to each other, they empower patients in different ways. By using EHR the patient can have access and knowledge of his/her health information while with PHR he/she is granted with administration privileges too.

Additional interesting ways to empower patients focus on translating the methodology of patient support groups to virtual world using social media and online communities where patient receives advice from peers and he/she can provide information for others.

Finally, other relevant technologies include the Internet as a source of information, software and mobile apps, security mechanisms, devices and communication media (such as traditional and IP telephony or email).

Having identified the technologies mostly used to empower patients, it is crucial to review/see how the different approaches empower patients. As a matter of fact, the same technology can deploy two different approaches for Patient Empowerment. For example, email communication could be used for strengthening doctor–patient relation or alerting patient of modification of his/her health information record. The most popular way for empowerment is patient education, shared for 40% of reviewed articles. It is widely argued that an educated patient can make more informed decisions, improve compliance, reduce anxiety levels and participate actively in the treatment of his/her diseases. This fact is more relevant in chronic scenarios where the patient must modify his/her life and adapt to permanent conditions. If healthy scenarios were considered, benefits of patient education could be translated to the maintenance of health and prevention tasks through citizen education. Enhancing commodity of patients is another important approach for empowerment.

It is accomplished by reducing the complexity of daily tasks such as the patient—doctor communication (e.g. email or instant messaging), online access to administrative services and tele-diagnosis.

Another relevant paradigm to empower patients is to turn them into providers of support and advice for peers. As providers, patients feel useful, and as receivers, they obtain support and comprehension of peers that suffer (or suffered) similar conditions.

Security also counts as a driving force for Patient Empowerment in different ways. Control of distribution and disclosure of personal information are the most relevant Patient Empowerment mechanisms followed by control over its edition, and privacy and confidentiality of communications. Due to the confidential content of health information, patients are very concerned with security requirements.

Other Patient Empowerment ways are to strengthen the doctor—patient relation, to access general or personalized information and to promote behavior modification, etc.

Patient empowerment implications on daily practice are restricted to modify attitudes of patients and not to involve them actively in processes.

As revolutionary technology in every sector of society, web services are also one of the most used technologies for empowering patients. Their application covers several approaches such as information web pages, interactive portals, infrastructure of distributed services and remote data access. Their versatility, popularity and development in other domains make them the first choice for developers of solutions in health domain.

Booming technologies in other sectors (e.g. social media and mobile apps) are being steadily applied to empower patients. Forums, blogs and social networks are suitable vehicles to translate support groups from real life to the electronic world, ease the communication among patients and professionals and strengthen the continuity of care beyond physical appointments. In addition, the wide adoption of smartphones in daily life brings many potential trends for patient empowerment such as ubiquitous access to health information for patients and professionals or smartphone applications for monitoring chronic conditions, disease prevention tasks and promotion of healthy habits.

Finally, an interesting result is the slightly higher use of PHR (12.7% of articles) for empowering patients than of EHR (10%).

From Jorge Calvillo et al.'s literature review, we can conclude that different levels of empowerment exist. All the reviewed approaches have the same objective (i.e. to empower patients), but the grade of autonomy or involvement that the subject obtains varies from one solution to another.

Obstacles to the effective patient empowerment abound. First, in order to play their proactive roles, patients must able to trust in technology empowering them. Second, another critical obstacle is reluctance of doctors to lose their power.

Thus, involved actors' attitudes toward Patient Empowerment will determine the real swift of healthcare delivery models and the role of each actor. If obstacles and gaps are successfully addressed, at medium-term technology will ease the emergence of a new patient fully equipped for the healthcare challenging scenarios of the twenty-first century.

Patient empowerment: A process or an outcome?

Empowerment, by definition, is a *social* process, since it occurs in relationship to others. It is a *process* similar to a path or journey, one that develops as we work through it. Aujoulat, Marcolongo, Bonadiman and Deccache

(2008)[12] define patient empowerment as a process. According to them, patient empowerment is

> a process of personal transformation which occurs through a double process of 1) "holding on" to previous self-representations and roles and learning to control the disease and treatment, so as to differentiate one's self from illness on the one hand, and on the other hand 2) "letting go," by accepting to relinquish control, so as to integrate illness and illness-driven boundaries as being part of a reconciled self.

Other authors, with whom I strongly agree, have described patient empowerment as both a process and an outcome. For instance, Funnel, Anderson, Arnold, Barr, Donnelly, Johnson, Taylor-Moon, and White (1991)[13] emphasized that while empowerment can be seen as "the process of discovery and development of one's inherent capacity to be responsible for one's life," they pointed out that "patient empowerment is fundamentally an outcome." Therefore, patients are empowered "when they have the knowledge, skills, attitudes, and self-awareness necessary to improve the quality of their lives."

Anderson and Fannell (2010)[14] define patient empowerment as "a process designed to facilitate self-directed behaviour change." Based on this definition, patient empowerment is linked to the internal motivation of patients to change the way they deal with their disease / condition, rather than external motivation—for instance by healthcare professionals—in order to increase patients' adherence to treatments and advices.

Anderson and Funnell (2010)[15] state that patient empowerment starts when healthcare professionals acknowledge that patients are in control of their lives and healthcare services they use. They further claim that empowerment occurs:

1. when healthcare professionals aim "to increase the capacity of patients to think critically and make autonomous, informed decisions" (*empowerment as a process*); and
2. when patients actually make informed and autonomous decisions about their healthcare management (*empowerment as an outcome*) (Anderson and Funnell 2010: 277)[16].

Relying on a considerable literature review, and considering patient empowerment as a multidimensional concept, Ouschan et al. (2008)[17] have developed a three-dimensional framework to define a set of patient empowerment guidelines focusing on patients with chronic illness conditions. They use the dimension "patient control" when the patient acquires an increased confidence in being

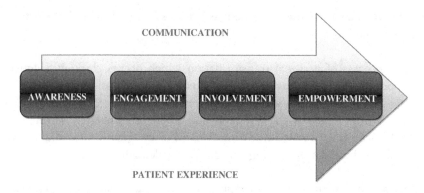

Figure 1.3 Empowerment continuum

in control of his/her disease, managing treatment administration, along with disease-related anxiety and the *"patient participation"* dimension to evaluate the patient's level of participation, the different role of the patient during medical interview and other types of interactions with physicians. Finally, they use the physician support dimension to discuss the support and/or education the patient receives from physicians.

The *"support"* empowerment dimension highlights how important and needed it is that physicians effectively communicate with patients using an approach aiming at motivating and encouraging them to become "empowered." Patient empowerment will occur only if physicians are willing to support the patient throughout the *"empowering process."*

For the aim of this book we are going to consider the following continuum from awareness to empowerment where communication, patient experience and physician's role play a central role (Figure 1.3).

It starts with creating awareness as knowledge or perception of a situation or fact capable to generate engagement in one's own health, care and treatment.

The success of *engagement* lies in empowerment. It isn't just about health outcomes; patient empowerment also improves engagement between providers and patients, encouraging better communication and limiting the chances of misdiagnosis.

The success of a patient engagement tool such as a patient portal, for instance, is solely determined by patients using it. In order for them to do that, there needs to be *transparency in the information conveyed* to them, in order for them to make informed decisions with their physicians and health providers. Thus empowering patients with the right information about their health, ways to care for themselves and sharing information regarding their treatment will succeed in ensuring continued engagement with physicians. Doing this is likely to promote a meaningful use of a patient engagement portal.

In addition to engagement we also need to generate *involvement*. Patient involvement means involvement in the design, planning and delivery of health services. As a result of these *three steps* we pursue patient empowerment as the process in which patients understand their role, are given the knowledge and skills by their healthcare provider to perform a task in an environment that recognizes community and cultural differences and encourages patient participation.[18]

The role of physicians in patient empowerment

"What needs to happen is for doctors to come down off their pedestal and for patients to get up off their knees," said Robert Johnstone of the International Alliance of Patient Organizations at the First European Conference on Patient Empowerment held in Copenhagen, Denmark on April 11–12, 2012.

Over the last few years many times I have been wondering how much is the physician's fault and if there are probably a number of variables which are not in the hands of the physicians that need to be identified and managed by both physicians and non-physicians for patient empowerment to produce the expected outcomes.

At this aim, let's see what is the psychology behind patient empowerment and the physicians' role.

A patient is constantly making decisions with regards to care. It begins with how they interpret symptoms such as whether that persistent pain is circumstantial or worthy of medical attention. In deciding treatment options, patients make the most explicit choice based on information they have gathered. Finally, there is the treatment phase where a patient must be committed to treatment.[19] This means that there are three characteristic situations where a patient must make decisions: observation of state of health before presenting to a HCP, discussion and decision during the medical interview, and the treatment phase.

During the observation phase, the patient passively observes his/her health, noting any points of concern, monitoring them and choosing between seeking medical attention or not. The first patient decision relates to symptom observation. Cognitive psychology defines a confirmation bias as "a tendency to search for information that confirms one's preconceptions."[20] A hypochondriac patient is subject to this bias when they interpret benign symptoms to be caused by a serious disease. Working in the other direction, another patient may look for days when they feel good to confirm that they are healthy. This bias toward desirable outcomes is consistent with the desirability bias, a form of "wishful thinking."[21] Another form of bias is the denial bias. A study by Phelan et al. (1992) showed that there was "widespread denial" among women who were late to seek medical attention for breast cancer.[22] While these psychological phenomena are challenges at the micro level, they are also challenges that must be met at the population level. Much of the observation takes place with no physician involvement whatsoever. Because this observation phase is often free of physician involvement, these biases must not only be confronted during face-to-face contact with HCPs, but at every point in the interface between the health care body and the general public.

To counter these biases, health managers must focus on communication that manipulates another bias of cognitive psychology, known as the framing bias. A frame is defined as "a psychological device that offers a perspective and manipulates salience in order to influence subsequent judgment." In a landmark study by Beth Meyerowitz and Shelly Cheiken (1987), it was shown that framing—manipulated through language—significantly affected the intentions of young women to perform breast self-examinations (BSE).[23] They distributed three different pamphlets about BSE, loss-frame, gain-frame and no-arguments, where the frame type is defined by whether the negative consequences of not performing BSEs (loss-frame), the positive benefits of performing BSEs (gain-frame) or neither (no-arguments) were stressed. After four months, 57% of subjects in the loss-frame pool increased the frequency of BSE compared to that prior to reading the pamphlet, while 38% and 39% reported the same for the gain-frame and no-arguments pamphlet. This shows that health managers must be especially mindful of the psychological implications of the conversations they are having with the patients, at both the micro and macro levels.

The second characteristic situation where a patient must make decisions is during the medical interview which involves two components. In the first, a patient and their HCPs discuss the medical elements of the condition, as well as treatment options and risks. This phase can be considered one of information gathering in essence and similar to the observation phase, though ideally it is less autonomous as it is a process done in partnership with the guidance of an HCP. The same cast of biases can apply here too, as a patient may have confirmation, desirability and other similar biases that will direct their focus to and from certain bits of information.

The decision-making process can be influenced by several biases such as the focusing effect, defined as "not taking into account alternatives to an option that has been initially proposed or generated,"[24] loss aversion which refers to the concept that people are more motivated to avoid losses than pursue equal gains (i.e. when considering serious risks from surgery) and availability heuristic which is employed when a person "estimates frequency or probability by the ease with which instances or associations could be brought to mind." As with loss aversion, it remains the responsibility of HCPs to notice these heuristics and manage them. This takes time and will likely cause tensions in the patient-HCP relationship, but it is nonetheless a necessary component of good patient-centered healthcare. To counter the focus effect, the exploration of alternative options must be facilitated under the guidance of HCPs.

Finally, a patient must make decisions at the treatment stage. The compliance of patients to the treatments prescribed is unfortunately often very low. While non-compliance is brought about by poor education regarding the disease and its treatment timeline, it is made worse by the fact that patients may deny that they are sick, or be overconfident regarding their health. These are HCP-independent processes, and are good arguments for increasing the frequency of HCP-patient interactions, discussions about patients' concerns and beliefs, and patient education. For treatments that take place over extended periods of time, particularly those that include asymptomatic phases, patients must be closely monitored to facilitate discussion with HCPs. Unfortunately, many of these thoughts and emotions are tied to external perceptions and stigma, meaning that the scope of the education efforts is widened from being patient-specific to community-wide.

Having clarified the psychology behind patient empowerment we might say that physician's role is to put the patient's specific case in context and to rank choices in a realistic way to balance risk and benefit.

Probably one of the biggest issues with effective patient empowerment has to do with the changing dynamic of the medical conservation. Once upon a time, in the paternal days of medical care, the physician decided for patients, as he would decide for his own children.[25]

The movement toward individual patient empowerment has changed the tone and balance of the conversation. The physician is no longer the final decision maker, if really he ever was. He/she is adviser, educator and guide. He is not the pilot; he is the assistant navigator. The captain patient decides not only destination, but also the journey's path.

For certain doctors, at certain times, this change in how information is shared and decisions made, may sound like the patient is not listening. The physician may feel superfluous or disrespected. Most probably this is a failure of the physician to understand the dynamic of "modern" medical conversation. The patient means no disrespect, but may automatically feel in change.

Decision-making and independence are absolute requirements for the patient. Still, the physician needs to educate, support, and always stay near, ready to advise or catch the patient if they begin to fall.

Every relationship between every patient and every physician is different and changes continuously. There are times when the physician is absolutely in control, such as in medical extremis or in the operating room. At other moments, the patient must stand completely alone. Some patients want or need more control, and others less. Families are part of the control matrix. On-going changes in a patient's health alter how information and decision-making flows.

Physicians must understand that medical decisions are about the patient, and not feel threatened, guilty or confused.

The main barriers to physician's empowerment

Digital technologies provide a way for populations to access care outside of traditional, in-person care models. Telemedicine, for example, empowers patients via convenient and direct access to providers. E-visits allow consumers to get medical advice from the comfort of their own homes. Digital monitoring tools allow consumers to conveniently self-monitor health conditions in conjunction with providers, empowering them to be involved in their own care.

Expanding the use of digital health technologies can also produce significant cost savings for the healthcare sector. A recent study found that the cost of four days of in-hospital heart monitoring could be reduced by up to 72% through the use of telemedicine and remote monitoring. Clearly, digital technologies that connect providers and consumers provide significant benefits to stakeholders across the health industry.

As the healthcare system has evolved, so have patient and provider preferences for care. In order for digital technologies to be widely adopted and effectively leveraged, both patient and provider buy-in is necessary.

A recent study[26] suggests that our journey has already started:

- Nearly 50% of consumers and 79% of physicians believe that the use of mobile devices can help clinicians better coordinate care.
- Nearly 50% of consumers said that they would be willing to communicate with their caregivers online.
- 53% of clinicians said that they would be comfortable with patients checking vital signs with a device on their phones.

To get a better understanding of the perceptions about the use of health digital technologies, HRI conducted a survey of 1,000 primary care physicians, physicians specializing in chronic disease, and physician "extenders" (e.g. nurse practitioners and physician's assistants). HRI also interviewed more than 25 industry professionals, including board and leadership members of the eHealth Initiative based in Washington, DC. They found that there is room for digital technology to make clinicians more efficient caregivers.

But there's work to be done. Only 15% of clinicians report that they currently offer telehealth services to patients with chronic conditions. While another 28% said they are considering such services, only half of physicians who are conducting e-visits are getting paid for at least some of them.

Based on the results of a survey realized in August 2016 by Medscape (1,423 healthcare providers, including 847 physicians, and 1,103 patients were interviewed) physicians and patients disagree widely on how much access patients should have to *physician notes*. Even so, 6 of 10 physicians felt that patients have the right to see all physician notes.[27]

Since 2014, patients have become significantly more comfortable with the *security* of digital health technology and electronic health records (EHRs). However, despite the near-universal adoption of EHRs in physician practices—in a recent Medscape survey,[28] 91% of physicians said they were currently using an EHR—physicians have not grown more comfortable with the security and privacy of digital health technology over the past two years.

Patients were significantly more likely to agree that using an electronic patient portal to communicate with their physician was beneficial. Despite patients' relatively greater support of such portals, there isn't consistent evidence that using a patient portal translates to better care or patient outcomes. A 2013 review[29] that included 14 randomized controlled trials found that "there was no consistent evidence that access to a patient portal significantly improved clinical outcome, satisfaction or adherence to treatment."

One of the most significant differences between patients and physicians was in their perception of how EHRs affect a practice. EHRs are often touted as a way to improve practice efficiency, and an overwhelming majority of patients—four out of every five—believe that EHRs help physicians and their staffs work more efficiently.

However, many physicians saw EHRs quite differently—about one out of every two physicians reported that EHRs either made no difference or reduced their efficiency. These results mirror those reported in a recently published, separate Medscape survey specifically on EHRs.[30] In that survey, a majority of physicians reported a reduced overall workflow with EHRs, and a majority also reported that EHRs decreased the amount of face-to-face time they had with patients.

Indeed, despite the promise that electronic health records would cut billing costs, savings have yet to materialize, according to a major new study conducted by researchers at Harvard Business School and Duke University in 2016 and 2017. They found that despite the fact that Duke has an established electronic health record (EHR) system and an efficient, centralized billing department, generating a single bill cost anywhere from $20 to $215 depending on the type of visit. In fact, while automation may help on some record-keeping tasks, it also imposes its own costs. "In fact, more costs were shifted over to doctors in that they had to enter more codes into the so-called automated system," Kaplan says. "Turns out that that gets them annoyed, and it distracts them from dealing with the patient." The study looked at five types of visits: primary care visits, ER visits resulting in a patient discharge, general medicine hospital stays, outpatient surgical procedures, and inpatient surgeries.[31]

Main findings included:

- A primary care visit necessitated 13 minutes in billing and insurance-related activities, costing $20. The time and cost ramped up to 100 minutes and $215 for an inpatient surgery.
- Just the physicians' portion of the time and cost spent on billing amounted to 3 minutes and about $6 for a primary care visit, up to 15 minutes and $51 for surgery.
- Physicians, who cost between $3 and $8 per minute, are doing administrative tasks that a scribe costing 50 cents a minute could do better, Kaplan says.

Patients and physicians showed similar levels of support for new approaches to delivering and receiving patient care, such as telemedicine and "doctor on demand" apps for smartphones and tablets.

Telemedicine apps, which offer on-demand video consultations with a physician or nurse, are growing rapidly. Some of the more popular apps include Doctor on Demand, which is backed by Google and the television personality Phil McGraw; Teladoc; MDLive; American Well; and KRY, the Swedish video-based healthcare provider.

Physicians overestimated patients' preference for in-office visits. Whereas 68% of patients said they preferred to see a doctor in person, 81% of physicians said they believed patients preferred to see them in person.

Unlike questions related to patient portals or patients' access to physician notes, there was strong agreement by physicians of all ages as well as among specialists vs primary care physicians—a strong majority felt that patients preferred to see them in person.

Despite the difference, the overall results suggest that both patients and physicians continue to value an in-person appointment, even as telemedicine technologies gradually become more available.

In terms of barriers to using telemedicine, patients and physicians expressed concerns that were unique to their perspective in the patient/physician interaction. Patients were most concerned about receiving an accurate diagnosis. The current lack of access to telemedicine was also perceived as a significant barrier.

Among physicians, practice issues were most important. Malpractice and liability concerns ranked highest among physicians. Reimbursement for physicians' time and effort ranked second, although technical problems and privacy/security issues were also seen as significant barriers for many physicians.

For physicians, perceived barriers to telemedicine varied depending on whether they practiced in an urban, suburban or rural area. Physicians in urban and suburban practices were most concerned about malpractice liability, reflecting the overall trend; in contrast, physicians in rural practices felt that technical problems with telemedicine technology were a greater obstacle.

Whereas about one-third of physicians reported that they are excited about new technologies in medicine, the majority of physicians—about three in five—view incorporating new technologies into their practice as an obligation. In other words, they see it as a mandate by hospital administrators or a requirement to attest for meaningful use, or simply to stay current with practice standards.

Physicians' attitudes toward technology correlated with their age. The greatest proportion of physicians who felt that technology was exciting and use it as often as possible were younger than 35 years; in contrast, the greatest proportion of physicians who felt that technology was "a bit beyond me" were older than 55 years.

Finally, based on the results of the Web in Salute—FADOI survey (2018),[32] conducted in Italy with the Association of Internists (FADOI), physicians are not sure or don't think that digital tools used for patient empowerment reduce the time of the medical interview (32% and 37% respectively) or improve healthcare outcomes (38% and 12% respectively), while 49% of respondents agree that digital tools can improve healthcare outcomes. In addition physicians report that the main barriers to the successful patient empowerment with digital tools is the lack of clinic evidence (42%) or a certification from an independent scientific society or institution (30%) as long as the lack of their organization support (42%).

Clearly, a majority of healthcare consumers and providers are interested in using new digital technologies. However, in our current healthcare systems, there are numerous barriers to doing so, from regulatory issues to reimbursement challenges to consumer and provider knowledge gaps.

Overcoming barriers to the widespread adoption of digital technologies could be a key way to improve access to healthcare, and subsequently health outcomes.

"Physicians play a central role in successfully empowering patients."

Notes

1 David J. Cook, Jeffrey E. Thompson, Joseph A. Dearani and Sharon K. Prinsen (2014), "How Mayo Clinic is using iPads to empower patients." *Harvard Business Review.*

2 R.M. Anderson and M.M. Funnell (2010), "Patient empowerment: myths and misconceptions." *Patient Educ Couns.*, 79(3), 277–282. doi:10.1016/j.pec.2009.07.025.

3 G. Laverack (2005), *Public Health: Power, Empowerment and Professional Practice.* Basingstoke: Palgrave Macmillan.

4 José Luis Monteagudo Peña and Oscar Moreno Gil (2007), *e-Health for patient empowerment in Europe.* Madrid: Ministerio de Sanidad y Consumo.

5 Nanette Page and Cheryl E. Czuba (1999), "Empowerment: What is it?" *Journal of Extension*, 37(5).

6 G. Laverack (2005), *Public Health: Power, Empowerment and Professional Practice.* Basingstoke: Palgrave Macmillan.

7 Axel Helmer et al. (2011), "Empowering patients through personal health records: A survey of existing third-Party web-based PHR products." *e-Journal of Health Informatics*, 6(3).

8 Jorge Calvillo et al. (2013), "How technology is empowering patients? A literature review." *Health Expectations*, 18, 643–652.

9 WHO website.

10 World Health Organization (2009), "WHO guidelines on hand hygiene in health care: First global patient safety challenge clean care is safer care." [online]. Available at https://www.ncbi.nlm.nih.gov/books/NBK144022/ [Accessed 12 January 2018].

11 Jorge Calvillo et al. (2013), "How technology is empowering patients? A literature review." *Health Expectations*, 18, 643–652.

12 Isabelle Aujoulat, Renzo Marcolongo, Leopoldo Bonadiman, and Alain Deccache (2008), "Reconsidering patient empowerment in chronic illness: A critique of models of selfefficacy and bodily control." *Social Science & Medicine* 66, 1228–1239.

13 M.M. Funnell, R.M. Anderson, M.S. Arnold, P.A Barr, M. Donnelly, P.D. Johnson, et al. (1991), "Empowerment: An idea whose time has come in diabetes education." *Diabetes Educ.* 17, 37–41.

14 R.M. Anderson, M.M. Funnell (2010), "Patient empowerment: myths and misconceptions." *Patient Educ Couns.*, 79(3), 277–282. doi:10.1016/j.pec.2009.07.025.

15 R.M. Anderson, M.M. Funnell (2010), "Patient empowerment: myths and misconceptions." *Patient Educ Couns.*, 79(3), 277–282. doi:10.1016/j.pec.2009.07.025.

16 R.M. Anderson and M.M. Funnell (2010), "Patient empowerment: myths and misconceptions." *Patient Educ Couns.*, 79(3), 277–282. doi:10.1016/j.pec.2009.07.025.

17 Ouschan-Macrae, Robyn, Jillian C.D. Sweeney, and Lester W. Johnson (2003), *The Dimensions of Patient Empowerment in the Context of Chronic Illness Consultations. 2003 World Marketing Congress.* Perth, WA: Academy of Marketing Science. [online]. Available at https://espace.curtin.edu.au/handle/20.500.11937/44142 [Accessed March 6, 2018].

18 World Health Organization (2009), "WHO guidelines on hand hygiene in health care: First global patient safety challenge clean care is safer care." [online]. Available at https://www.ncbi.nlm.nih.gov/books/NBK144022/ [Accessed January 12, 2018].

19 I. Shahin (2008), "Managing the psychology of health care: What it means and what it is worth." *McGill Journal of Medicine*, 11(2), 191–198.

20 D. Myers (2001), *Social Psychology*, 7th edition. New York: McGraw-Hill.

21 Z. Krizan and P. Windschitl (2007), "The influence of outcome desirability on optimism." *Psychological Bulletin*, 133(1), 95–121.

22 M. Phelan, M. Dobbs and A.S. David 1992, "'I thought it would go away': Patient denial in breast cancer." *Journal of the Royal Society of Medicine*, 85, 206–207. [PMC free article] [PubMed].

23 B. Meyerowitz and S. Chaiken (1987), "The effect of message framing on breast self-examination attitudes, intentions, and behavior." *Journal of Personality and Social Psychology*, 52(3), 500–510.

24 F. Del Missier, D. Ferrante, and E. Costantini (2006), "Focusing effects in predecisional information acquisition." *Acta Psychologica*, 125(2), 155–174.

25 James C. Salwitz (2015), "Patient empowerment: Scaffolding has a place in health care." [online]. Available at https://www.kevinmd.com/blog/2015/09/patient-empowerment-scaffolding-has-a-place-in-health-care.html [Accessed March 6, 2018].

26 PwC's Health Research Institute (2014), "Healthcare delivery of the future: How digital technology can bridge time and distance between clinicians and consumers." [online]. Available at https://www.pwc.com/us/en/health-industries/top-health-industry-issues/assets/pwc-healthcare-delivery-of-the-future.pdf [Accessed on March 6, 2018].

27 Gabriel Miller (2016), "Physician and patient attitudes toward technology in medicine." [online]. Available at https://www.medscape.com/features/slideshow/public/technology-in-medicine [Accessed on March 6, 2018].

28 C. Peckham, L. Kane and S. Rosensteel (2016), "Medscape EHR report 2016: Physicians rate top EHRs." *Medscape News & Perspective*, August 25. www.medscape.com/features/slideshow/public/ehr2016 [Accessed September 14, 2016].

29 C.L. Goldzweig, G. Orshansky, N.M. Paige et al. (2013), "Electronic patient portals: Evidence on health outcomes, satisfaction, efficiency, and attitudes: A systematic review." *Ann Intern Med*, 159, 677–687.

30 C. Peckham, L. Kane and S. Rosensteel (2016), "Medscape EHR report 2016: Physicians rate top EHRs." *Medscape News & Perspective*, August 25. www.medscape.com/features/slideshow/public/ehr2016 [Accessed September 14, 2016].

31 Roberta Holland (2018), "Electronic health records were supposed to cut medical costs. They haven't." *Harvard Business Review*.

32 Letizia Affinito (2018), "Web in salute, independent survey conducted in partnership with FADOI - Scientific Society of Internal Medicine." Based on the results of the Web in Salute survey conducted in Italy with the Association of Internists (FADOI) in combination with clinical evidence (52%) and reimbursement (39%), physician and patient involvement in the new technology design could positively contribute to increase and improve the efficacy of digital tools to empower the patient (35% and 30% respectively). What is still missing to allow a better and more effective patient empowerment with digital tools along with clinical evidence (42%), organization's support (42%), certification from scientific institutions and associations (30%), training (43%), and culture (36%) is both the availability of tools designed around physicians (15%) and patients' needs (24%).

Physicians' reluctance to engage with technology

2

Most companies do not succeed in their efforts to adopt new technology because they merely import their digital tools in the healthcare setting and in the physician's hands. In this chapter we are going to explore what is the primary advantage of a patient–physician digital strategy over a purely digital one and how developing a successful strategy can help organizations form and strengthen relationships with both physicians and patients in ways that also benefit the organization. We'll begin our journey with a **literature review** on the adoption of telemedicine in action with a main focus on participation in telemedicine and the perception of its usefulness.

According to a study by Maria Dolors Ruiz Morilla et al. (2017),[1] physicians considered telemedicine (TM) to be useful, especially those with previous experience with this technology. The attitude of healthcare professionals toward TM is a facilitating factor for the implementation of this type of project. Physicians favor the incorporation of technology into their daily lives provided that these innovations are useful.[2] Similar to previous studies,[3] the results of their study conclude that having participated in a TM project is one of the factors that most influences physicians' opinions of TM, resulting in a more positive view. In addition, although these professionals do not perceive more needs or difficulties than those who are not familiar with TM, they do perceive greater benefits with its use. It was of note that they considered that TM would improve the quality of clinical practice, patient health, and the professional workload. Nevertheless, they did demand projects with adequate funding. This can be explained in that the efficiency of some of these programs is not clear.[4,5] Indeed, many pilot programs have not been implemented because of the lack of an economic feasibility plan associated with the study.[6] The ease of-use of the electronic devices was of particular concern as was the need for incentives to use the technology.

Professionals also demanded adequate technological teams and specific training in order to improve their technological skills. The main threat was considered to be the patients' preference for in-person visits, perhaps in concordance with the classical view of the physician–patient relationship. The results of this study demonstrate the different view of the implementers, whose priorities differ from those of clinicians which are more related to efficiency.

This is important for the implementation of TM since it is the implementers who decide as to the economic feasibility and project funding and how the project will be executed. In order to generalize the use of TM the view of the implementers must be combined with that of the professionals taking into account the needs of the clinicians and their participation in the decision-making progress.[7,8] Professionals working in private healthcare consider that TM will provide greater benefits, as long as that the system is easy for their patients to use and incentives for its use are available. To this end, it is necessary to address the payment method for electronic visits in healthcare systems, since this factor may limit generalized use of TM.

The disassociation between professional and personal use of the Internet was also of note. That is, the profile of an Internet user did not condition how they used the Internet in the workplace or their opinion of TM. This is surprising, since according to the classical study by Rogers,[9] and confirmed by Zanaboni in a study on the use of technology in health,[10] the type of user is usually described according to at what time on the S-shaped logistic growth curve the user adopts the technology. We'll see more about this topic in Chapter 6, dedicated to adoption and diffusion of new digital tools.

Nevertheless, authors' findings suggest that it should be taken into account that a single user may have two roles, depending on whether we study their private or professional profile.

This disassociation between the personal and professional use of new technologies might initially seem paradoxical, but it may demonstrate the degree to which technology has entered into the private life of professionals. Nevertheless, there has been no change in the classical physician–patient relationship. That is, professionals have begun to see their world as being 2.0, but they still need to modify the way they work with their patients, and incorporate new technological tools.[11] Therefore, although professionals have adopted the Internet for their personal use and consider it very important for their work, they do not feel that the health of their patients is affected by the use or not of the Internet to seek information related to healthcare.

With regard to the professional use of the Internet, although electronic communication between professionals does take place, it is not used to keep in contact with patients. On the other hand, physicians use very few medical applications compared with their use of other apps, and consequently do not recommend these tools to their patients. There is little evidence of why this occurs, but it is likely that the lack of scientific evidence demonstrating their use[12] plays an important role in whether or not health-related apps are prescribed.

In relation to the personal use of the Internet, having a tablet is related to having a 2.0 attitude; that is, more intensive use of social networks. On the other hand, it is of note that having a smartphone does not determine how the Internet is used, probably because of their generalized use among the population, with most professionals having access to a telephone with a connection to the Internet. Indeed, authors found a relationship between having a tablet and making greater use of the Internet and being more likely to use new technologies in clinical practice.

Professionals working in private healthcare communicate more with their patients over the Internet, probably in order to provide more services. On the other hand, this communication is less frequent than that of professionals in the public health system in which an internal network facilitates communication.

The 2.0 philosophy has been incorporated into many areas of our lives, but healthcare systems still have a long way to go in order to incorporate this new way of understanding the relationship between the patient, their health and their disease. The classical physician–patient relationship needs to evolve. Only in doing so will health professionals feel comfortable incorporating technology into how they interact with patients.

New technologies adoption by physicians

As previously highlighted, a number of studies show positive evidence with regard to the adoption of digital tools to empower patients. This optimistic evidence has encouraged the implementation of e-health technology worldwide, guaranteeing the commitment of governments such as the US and a number of countries in Europe to allot a significant amount of resources to promote e-health technology. However, despite the high investment on e-health technology by healthcare systems, the evidence of the effects of e-health benefits is still very poor. In some instances, the lack of systems structures (e.g., integration of e-health systems) presents a barrier to the adoption of the new technology, while in other cases it can be detrimental. In addition, the uptake and adoption of e-health technologies has not always been consistent within healthcare practice, and adoption of these technologies has lagged behind.[13]

Physicians' acceptance of e-health technology is critical, consequently it is important to identify influences that delay the uptake in order to overcome it.

Based on the results of a scoping review realized by Chloe de Grood et al. (2016),[14] aiming at summarizing the current literature identifying barriers and opportunities that facilitate adoption of e-health technology by physicians, a number of *barriers* and *facilitators* to the adoption of e-health technology by physicians can be identified.

Among the main themes, threatened clinical autonomy, cost and liability issues, and training and support were the most cited.

Boonstra and Broekhuis,[15] Castillo et al.[16] Gagnon et al.[17] and Goldstein et al.[18] support these findings. They found that the most cited barriers to EMR adoption as financial, lack of time, and technical barriers. Boonstra and Broekhuis[19] identified these most cited barriers as *"primary"* barriers, given that such barriers are first to arise with the adoption process of EMR. Other factors that need to be addressed are motivation to adopt e-health technology, patient–physician interaction, training and support, system factors and threatened autonomy.

One of the main themes that became apparent was the threatened clinical autonomy. This may be due to multiple factors such as the physicians' desire to autonomously form their own clinical decisions without information provided by e-health technology, fear of change, age, unwillingness to adopt, and limitation in time and effort.

Walter and Lopez[20] defined professional autonomy as "professionals" having control over the conditions, processes, procedures, or content of their work according to their own collective and, ultimately, individual judgment in the application of their profession's body of knowledge and expertise professional privacy. They found that threatened professional autonomy negatively affected perceived usefulness and the intention to use e-health technology.[21]

The *second* main theme that arose was cost and liability issues associated with the adoption of e-health technology by physicians. Concerns regarding reimbursement were the most cited within this theme. Physicians were less willing to utilize e-health technology with no reimbursement initiatives present.

The *third* main theme that arose in this study was the barriers surrounding training and support. Poor services from the vendor such as poor training and support for problems associated with the e-health technology and poor follow-up are barriers to the adoption of such devices. This is further complicated given that physicians are not technical experts and the systems are inherently complicated.

In order to further facilitate the adoption of e-health technology, physicians need the technology to be tailored to the individuals' knowledge of the e-health technology. Furthermore, "on-site experts" who are able to provide first-line support were highly encouraged. We'll see more about this topic in Chapter 6.

Lastly, follow-up sessions were considered an important factor contributing to the adoption of e-health technology.

Addressing barriers to the implementation of e-health technology is a complex process that requires support from health services authority, insurance companies, vendors, patients and physicians. The findings of this scoping review suggest that not all barriers are present in all practices. It is important for policy makers and hospital or practice managers to understand the specific barriers that challenge the practicing physicians and design appropriate interventions to address barriers and promote facilitating factors. This may be achieved through running in-depth interviews with the users, in this case physicians, to learn which are the specific barriers.

As anticipated, researchers and policymakers recognize the importance of having an evidence-based measurement of patient engagement, as it is a necessary tool for planning and implementing initiatives. However, with very few studies and limited data available, there is a lack of clearly defined evidence-based guidelines available which represents a critical barrier to physicians' adoption.

Based on the results of the Web in Salute - FADOI[22] survey (2018), conducted in Italy with the Association of Internists (FADOI), in combination with clinical evidence (52%) and reimbursement (39%), physician and patient involvement in the new technology design could positively contribute to increase and improve the efficacy of digital tools to empower the patient (35% and 30% respectively). What is still missing to allow a better and more effective patient empowerment with digital tools along with clinical evidence (42%), organization's support (42%), certification from scientific institutions and associations (30%), training (43%), and culture (36%) is both the availability of tools designed around physicians' (15%) and patients' needs (24%).

To conclude, regardless increased investments and apparent commitment from organizations, I keep listening to physicians complaining about EHRs and digital technologies that are too hard to use or not helping them in their clinical practice. We're still at the state where technology often hurts rather than helps physicians provide better care, while regulations, in their current form slow them down.

Complaints abound in the industry talks; the good news is they're not describing problems we don't know how to solve. That's what should make us optimistic.

The primary advantage of a patient–physician digital strategy over a purely digital one

No matter the industry, customers expect personalized experiences that deliver answers and solutions fast. Today, patients expect the same level of engagement from their healthcare providers.

As a matter of fact, studies show that patient engagement increases when patients' interaction with their clinicians increases. As such, clinical leaders have a main role in promoting and making this interaction happen. Both as a patient and a healthcare professional I have experienced that the physicians who get the best results in terms of patient empowerment so long as patients' sense of "being in control" of their health are those that sit down and make their consultation a conversation. They listen to you, hear you, and then explain to you what is going to happen. Focusing on the right measures of patient satisfaction is critical to pursuing positive healthcare outcomes. Focusing exclusively on food taste and bed comfort doesn't generate good clinical outcomes. The right and quality amount a physician spends with his/her patients is a satisfying point instead.

Patient engagement means truly involving the patient in care processes. Healthcare transformation demands the imagination, insight and experience that clinical leaders bring to the table. For healthcare organizations to succeed, in the new era clinical leaders will need to be more creative, flexible and agile than ever before.

On the other hand, physicians have been challenged to provide better care at a lower cost. Add to this the fact that many physicians are overworked and continually asked to meet more mandates to receive their reimbursements, and the picture for them begins to look grim.

But physicians want to make things better—for their hospitals, their patients and themselves.

As health systems progress toward new care and payment models, the key to success is physician engagement, and, as we'll see in Chapter 3, it must be cultivated early and at the highest levels.

"If doctors aren't engaged, implementing critical programs and new initiatives becomes all the more difficult," says Toby Cosgrove, MD, chief executive officer of the Cleveland Clinic.

"When physicians are fully engaged, an environment of trust and a genuine sense of value can be established. For example, physicians will have a strong ability to practice at the top of their specialty and foster higher collegiality and collaboration. Ultimately, that is good for patients' experience as well."

Experience is what drives digital tools adoption for both physicians and patients, so in order for your physicians and patients to become adopters as long as advocates you need to deliver them that experience not only through your devices but also through effective and valuable services, communication tools and content. In order to design the experience expected by the patient we will need to discuss it with our patients and analyze their answers. One thing that we quickly learn is that their perception of quality of care or innovation is perhaps not aligned with ours.

Many organizations make the mistake of paying more attention to the specific products they offer (that is, drugs, devices) than to the benefits and experiences produced by these products and the communication tools/activities developed for them. These organizations suffer from *marketing myopia*. They are so captured by their products that they focus only on existing wants and lose sight of underlying physicians'/patients' needs. They forget that a product is only a tool to solve a patient problem.[23] A manufacturer of a cancer drug may think that the customer needs a drug. But what the patient really needs, besides healing from cancer, is quality of life, convenience, comfort, transparent information, support and reassurance.[24]

While there is a debate over the best and feasible measurements of patient experience and engagement, I still believe it is essential for clinicians to understand every aspect of how patients view their care.

It is critical to learn about what have been their feelings and even emotions about billing, the kindness of the receptionist, how the communication with the doctor was, and how easy and/or smooth it has been to access records through the portal. Every single detail counts to create a better experience and increase the possibilities of digital tools adoption and, consequently, patient empowerment.

What really matters, above all, is organizations' willingness and capability to act on what physicians and patients say.

Healthcare satisfaction data focuses, most of the time, exclusively on functional needs—and does not consider emotional needs. In order to create interest, healthcare managers must focus on both functional and emotional needs.

Focusing holistically and intimately on the patients, their families, and their referring physicians' experiences is central in building the kind of relationship required to engage them and generate value.

Understanding the entire patient journey is important in supporting people who, for example, go through compliance management programs. Having patient insights allows the creation of better apps, as well as a better integration of those apps into EMRs. There is quite a lot of variation in physicians enrolling patients in compliance management programs. One of the key things to change is knowing whether they ask the right questions, whether the app they're using has been incorporated into the workflow, whether it's easy to use, and so on. Once you know if there is a problem and where it is, you can bring in health technology specialists to help the group incorporate the app into the EMR, so it's easier to use and takes less of the physician's time. Simultaneously, you will develop the relationship among patients/carers, physicians, and your brand, required to engage all actors involved in the journey.

You will need to see things through someone else's eyes, and, consequently, to put yourself in that person's shoes. Toward this end, "experience mapping" can be a very useful tool to help hospitals and pharma/biomedical/life sciences organizations find out what patients really think and feel about their healthcare experience.[25]

A successful strategy is needed to form and strengthen relationships with both physicians and patients

In spite of large investments of management time and money, innovation remains a frustrating pursuit in many organizations. Innovation projects often fail, and leading innovators such as Polaroid, Nokia, Sun Microsystems, Yahoo and Hewlett-Packard struggle to sustain their performance. Why is it so hard? The problem with innovation improvement efforts is rooted in the lack of an innovation strategy, that is, a commitment to a set of coherent, mutually reinforcing policies or behaviors aimed at achieving a specific competitive goal (i.e. profits; healthcare outcomes). A good strategy promotes alignment among different groups and divisions within an organization, makes objectives and priorities clear, and help focus efforts around them. Without an innovation strategy, innovation improvement actions can easily become an assortment of a mix of publicized best practices. There is nothing wrong with best practices per se. The problem is that an organization's capacity for innovation stems from an innovation system defined as a coherent set of interdependent processes and structures which give direction on how the company searches for new problems and solutions, synthesize ideas into a business concept and product designs, and select which projects get funded. Individual best practices involve trade-offs while, at the same time adopting a specific practice often requires additional changes to the rest of the organization's innovation system. A company without an innovation strategy won't be able to make trade-off decisions and choose all the elements of the innovation system.

Finally, without an innovation strategy, different parts of an organization can easily end up pursuing conflicting priorities—even if there's a clear business strategy. Different perspectives are critical to successful innovation. But without a strategy to integrate and align those perspectives around common priorities, the power of diversity is blunted or, worse, becomes self-defeating.[26]

In Chapter 3 we are going to see how to develop a digital health strategy process and how to make it a shared process for physician's empowerment.

> "Physician engagement, cultivated early at the highest levels, is the key to success."

Notes

1 Maria Dolors Ruiz Morilla, Mireia Sans, Albert Casasa and Nuria Giménez (2017), "Implementing technology in healthcare: Insights from physicians." *BMC Medical Informatics and Decision Making*.
2 A.L. Brewster, L.A. Curry, E.J. Cherlin, K. Talbert-Slagle, L.I. Horwitz and E.H. Bradley (2015), "Integrating new practices: A qualitative study of how hospital innovations become routine." *Implement Sci.*, 10(168). doi:10.1186/s13012-015-0357-3.
3 M. Mullen-Fortino, J. DiMartino, L. Entrikin, S. Mulliner, C.W. Hanson and J.M. Kahn (2012), "Bedside nurses' perceptions of intensive care unit telemedicine." *Am J Crit Care.*, 21(24–32). doi:10.4037/ajcc2012801.
4 G. Kumar, D.M. Falk, R.S. Bonello, J.M. Kahn, E. Perencevich and P. Cram (2013), "The costs of critical care telemedicine programs: A systematic review and analysis." *Chest.*, 143(19–29). doi:10.1378/chest.11-3031.
5 G. Flodgren, A. Rachas, A.J. Farmer, M. Inzitari and S. Shepperd (2015), "Interactive telemedicine: Effects on professional practice and health care outcomes." *Cochrane Database of Systematic Reviews*, 9. Art. No.: CD002098. doi:10.1002/14651858.CD002098.pub2.
6 E.M. Brebner and J.A. Brebner (2001), "Implementation and evaluation of telemedicine for remote health-care-the European Northern Periphery Programme Project." *J TelemedTelecare.*, 7, Suppl. 1, 68–69.
7 M.-P. Gagnon, J. Duplantie, J.-P. Fortin and R. Landry (2006), "Implementing telehealth to support medical practice in rural/remote regions: What are the conditions for success?" *Implement Sci.*, 1(18). doi:10.1186/1748-5908-1-18.
8 J. Ross, F. Stevenson, R. Lau and E. Murray. (2016), "Factors that influence the implementation of e-health: A systematic review of systematic reviews (an update)." *Implement Sci.*, 11(146). doi:10.1186/s13012-016-0510-7.
9 E.M. Rogers (1983), *Diffusion of Innovations*. New York: The Free Press.
10 P. Zanaboni and R. Wootton (2012), "Adoption of telemedicine: from pilot stage to routine delivery." *BMC Med Informa Decis Making*, 12(1). doi:10.1186/1472-6947-12-1.
11 S.D. Dorn (2015), "Digital health: Hope, hype, and Amara's Law." *Gastroenterology*, 149, 516–552.
12 L.E. Burke, J. Ma, K.M.J. Azar et al. (2015), "Current science on consumer use of mobile health for cardiovascular disease prevention: A scientific statement from the American Heart Association." *Circulation*, 132, 1157–1213. doi:10.1161/CIR.0000000000000232.

13 S. Ajami, S. Ketabi, S. Saghaeian-Nejad et al. (2011), "Requirements and areas associated with readiness assessment of electronic health records implementation. "*J Health Admin.*, 14, 71–78.

14 Chloe de Grood, Aida Raissi, Yoojin Kwon and Maria Jose Santana (2016), "Adoption of e-health technology by physicians: A scoping review." *Journal of Multidisciplinary Healthcare.*

15 A. Boonstra and M. Broekhuis (2010), "Barriers to the acceptance of electronic medical records by physicians from systematic review to taxonomy and interventions." *BMC Health Serv Res.*, 10, 231.

16 V. Castillo, A. Martinez-Garcia and J. Pulido (2010), "A knowledge-based taxonomy of critical factors for adopting electronic health record systems by physicians: A systematic literature review." *BMC Med Inform Decis Mak.* 10, 60. [PMC free article].

17 M. Gagnon, M. Desmartis, M. Labrecque et al. (2010), "Implementation of an electronic medical record in family practice: A case study." *Inform Prim Care*, 18(1), 31–40.

18 D.H. Goldstein, R. Phelan, R. Wilson et al. (2014), "Brief review: Adoption of electronic medical records to enhance acute pain management." *Can J Anaesth.*, 61(2), 164–179.

19 A. Boonstra and M. Broekhuis.(2010), "Barriers to the acceptance of electronic medical records by physicians from systematic review to taxonomy and interventions." *BMC Health Serv Res.*, 10, 231. [PMC free article].

20 Z. Walter and M.S. Lopez (2008), "Physician acceptance of information technologies: Role of perceived threat to professional autonomy." *Decis Support Syst.* 2008(46), 206–215.

21 Z. Walter and M.S. Lopez (2008), "Physician acceptance of information technologies: Role of perceived threat to professional autonomy." *Decis Support Syst.* 2008(46), 206–215.

22 Letizia Affinito (2018), Web in salute, independent survey conducted in partnership with FADOI - Scientific Society of Internal Medicine.

23 P. Kotler and G. Armstrong (2014), *Principles of Marketing*, 15th edition. Harlow: Pearson Education.

24 Letizia Affinito and John Mark (2015), *Socialize Your Patient Engagement Strategy: How Social Media and Mobile Apps Can Boost Health Outcomes.* Abingdon: Routledge.

25 Letizia Affinito and John Mark (2015), *Socialize Your Patient Engagement Strategy: How Social Media and Mobile Apps Can Boost Health Outcomes.* Abingdon: Routledge.

26 Gary P. Pisano (2015), "You need an innovation strategy." *Harvard Business Review.*

Part II

Developing a clear and sustainable digital strategy

A simple model of the Digital Health Strategy Process

3

As anticipated in Chapter 2, having a shared strategy can highly contribute to successful physician-and-patient empowerment with digital tools.

In this chapter we will introduce a seven-step digital health strategy model aiming at creating value for both physicians, patients and healthcare systems. In the first six steps, healthcare organizations act to understand physicians, create physicians value and build strong physician relationships and collaborations. In the final step, organizations bring back the rewards of creating superior value. In fact, by creating value for physicians, they consequently capture value from them in the form of patient empowerment, healthcare outcomes and patient QOL. We'll also see how to make it a shared process for physician's empowerment. I'll present each step individually.

We'll begin our journey with a **leading case history** on physician-and-patient empowerment strategy in action at Cleveland Clinic. With its slogan "Every life deserves world-class care," the Cleveland Clinic in Ohio has staked out a distinctive role in consumercentric, innovative healthcare—including the development and use of medical IT. Founded in 1921, the clinic is known for its high standards of research and practice and its ongoing role in fostering innovation and reducing costs.[1]

CC's strategy—to transform healthcare and to be able to deliver greater value to patients over time—is closely tied to their effective adoption of information technology, which is critical in improving the actual outcomes that they can deliver to patients.

The key components of the Cleveland Clinic's care model are their focus on the patient first; their physician-led model of care; and the coordination of their services across a spectrum of related clinical specialties focused on the patient. Finally, CC's group culture is really the secret sauce. For 90 years, they have worked in a collaborative fashion, and that is the greatest challenge for healthcare in the twenty-first century.

What has been strategic about CC's application of technology is thinking about how they can use it to affect the care delivery model.

For example, as they were building their electronic medical record (EMR) system, which serves their physicians and nurses both in the physicians' offices and in the hospital, they also built tools for patients that allowed them to access that information from home. They built tools for those physicians whom they did not directly employ, and they thought about approaches to interoperability. This meant acquiring data that they didn't generate, but that they could take into their systems and then use to make the best possible decisions for the patients they care for. In that sense, IT is strategic, because it truly facilitates a new transformed care delivery model.

But *adoption* of new technology remains a challenge today. Their goal was to improve the process of care over time. They thought about the best sequence for implementing the technology so that it delivered the most value at each step. So unlike many organizations, they did not implement the hospital information system first, but rather they began with the largest part of their organization, which is the ambulatory practice. That way, they could put a lot of patient information into the EMRs. When it became time to move to the inpatient side, their physicians were already using the technology on the ambulatory side, and they could immediately see the value. They could see information that had been collected prior to the patient's admission.

They found that by adhering closely to their practice goals, and applying the technology in a sequence that added value for the caregivers, they could overcome many of the barriers to technology adoption.

Information exchange is the last mile in getting the most value out of EMR technology. Within an organization, you must be able to exchange information among departmental systems—like between a laboratory system and a radiology system—or from one site to another to provide value to patients.

Over the past few years, Martin Harris, MD, chief information officer, and his team have worked with technology companies like Microsoft to allow patients, at their direction, to pull information from their local market into accounts that they control. The patients can make independent decisions to move that information to the Cleveland Clinic, thereby completing the loop and making the information available so that their physicians can provide the best care. Their goal is not to dictate which information exchange the patient wants to use. They just want to be connected to any service that they find valuable. No matter what the service is, they all have one fundamental requirement, and that is that they maintain the security and confidentiality of the patient's information.

Information technology has now become the fastest-growing innovation area at the Cleveland Clinic, and they have been leading in that area. They've done a number of projects, including the information exchange projects. They have built analytic tools that allow them to begin thinking about not just one patient, but entire groups of patients who either have a similar illness or are receiving a similar surgical procedure, so that we can better understand the inputs to that process and the outcomes.

The other great advance that they're seeing is more engagement on the part of patients. They were one of the early adopters of personal health records, and now they have more than 300,000 patients who have access to basic information like their lab test results, what medications they're on, their allergy list, their medical problems, and even decision support tools like when they need their next mammogram. They use IT to allow the patient to get at that information in a self-service mode just like many other industries, and that's becoming an expectation.

How can other CIOs in the healthcare industry benefit from experiences at the Cleveland Clinic?

As Harris states, healthcare is in a period of rapid change, and for the next decade or so, health CIOs in particular must be prepared for that process. The industry is moving beyond concentrating on technology and administrative issues—registering patients, getting them scheduled, producing a bill. "Now we're in a period that I call clinical integration," states Harris,

> where we're deploying clinical tools that allow doctors to write notes in a computer, place orders, and see their results immediately. Soon we will enter a phase that I call operational integration, which will be the most challenging but also the most beneficial for patients. In this phase, you begin by setting the outcome that you'd like to accomplish, then find the process that you'd like to use to meet that outcome, and then tune the technology to ensure that you hit it in a repeatable and reliable fashion.

The challenge for healthcare CIOs is to move away from focusing on the technology to focus on the marriage between the outcomes and how the technology allows us to accomplish them. It's a matter of broadening our perspective, moving away from being purely a technology expert to being an outcomes-oriented technology expert.

Successful organizations providing products and services in the healthcare industry have one thing in common: just like CC, they are extremely patient-centered and greatly committed to innovating both internally and externally.

These companies share a commitment to developing and successfully implementing strategies designed around physicians and patients' needs. They encourage everyone in the organization to help develop lasting physician-and-patient relationships based on creating value.

For healthcare institutions and medical practices, successful patient empowerment relies not just on new technology but also on a cultural shift. As the industry adapts to these changes, providers and healthcare administration must be prepared to face obstacles such as:

- difficulty shifting behaviors;
- different communication preferences;
- lack of health information exchanges;
- technology ease of use;
- operational and implementation challenges;
- workforce reluctance.

The many benefits of new healthcare technology and patient empowerment have been proven to outweigh the costs and challenges of implementation. However, successful adaptation and cultural shifts rarely occur without obstacles. Also, one of the biggest challenges that remain is the implementation of effective evidence-based methods of measurement for patient empowerment.

Patient empowerment has emerged as one of the most interesting keywords used by health politicians, academics and practitioners in Europe and the US in recent years. But to prove that it is more than a keyword, patient empowerment needs to be put into practice to demonstrate that it really generates value. Most importantly, when dealing with new technologies, in order to effectively empower patients we first need to focus on successfully empowering physicians. Overall, empowerment can be seen as a philosophy or vision, as well as a strategy.

As a consequence, the Digital Health Strategy Process can be represented in a simple, seven-step model (Figure 3.1). In the first six steps, healthcare

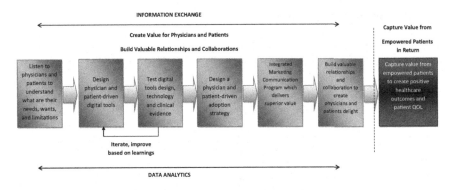

Figure 3.1 A simple model of the Digital Health Strategy Process

organizations act to understand physicians and patients, create physician-and-patient value and build strong physician-and-patient relationships. In the final step, organizations bring back the rewards of creating superior value. In fact, by creating value for physicians and patients, they consequently capture value from patients in the form of empowerment, improved health and healthcare outcomes.

Information exchange among all internal and external stakeholders and acquiring data for better decisions (data analytics) are two core aspects of this simple model.

In this chapter we will explore each step of this simple model of digital health strategy.

In this chapter we briefly review each step but focus more on the physician engagement and relationship steps—understanding physicians, building physician relationships, and capturing value from physicians. We'll look into the first, second, third and fourth steps more thoroughly in Chapters 4, 5, and 6.

Before illustrating it, let's clarify the concept of innovation value.

Executive teams' chronic problem is their emphasis on searching for breakthrough innovation which, almost by definition, is rare.

Breakthroughs may be worth pursuing, but most companies benefit more from incremental innovation efforts that add new forms of consumer value to their present products and services. The trick is to determine what elements to add in order to boost the perceived value of your offering. You don't want to expend resources adding features that consumers don't care about.

While what constitutes "value" can be nuanced and vary from person to person, Eric Almquist and his colleagues (2016), have identified 30 universal building blocks of value that meet fundamental human needs. These are basic

The Elements of Value Pyramid

Products and services deliver fundamental elements of value that address four kinds of needs: functional, emotional, life changing, and social impact. In general, the more elements provided, the greater customers' loyalty and the higher the company's sustained revenue growth.

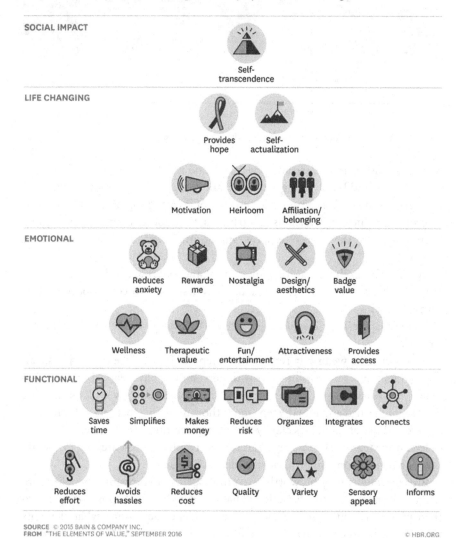

SOCIAL IMPACT

Self-transcendence

LIFE CHANGING

Provides hope   Self-actualization

Motivation   Heirloom   Affiliation/belonging

EMOTIONAL

Reduces anxiety   Rewards me   Nostalgia   Design/aesthetics   Badge value

Wellness   Therapeutic value   Fun/entertainment   Attractiveness   Provides access

FUNCTIONAL

Saves time   Simplifies   Makes money   Reduces risk   Organizes   Integrates   Connects

Reduces effort   Avoids hassles   Reduces cost   Quality   Variety   Sensory appeal   Informs

SOURCE © 2015 BAIN & COMPANY INC.
FROM "THE ELEMENTS OF VALUE," SEPTEMBER 2016

© HBR.ORG

Figure 3.2 The elements of Value Pyramid

attributes of a product or service that address four kinds of needs: function, emotion, life changes and social impact. Functional elements, for example, include saving time, reducing risk, and organizing. The pyramid shown in Figure 3.2 depicts how value elements fit into the four categories.[2]

Understanding physician's needs

Listening for physicians' digital and adoption needs, wants and limitations is an important first step. A serious Digital Health Strategy aiming at empowering patients must start with a comprehensive social media blueprint; that is, listening to the Internet, and not just your company website—the whole Internet.

The most significant thing that the health industry can do for a patient is to listen to what he/she and his/her physicians are saying and writing. We have already discussed how to listen to patients in "Socialize your patient engagement Strategy."[3] In this paragraph we'll focus exclusively on listening to physicians.

A growing number of physicians are using social media as a platform for health communication, but they do not use it entirely the same as others due to potential Privacy Rule violation concerns, and ultimately fear of potential repercussions a frank conversation could have on their real life. So how are doctors using social media? Are they using each platform in the same way? And what kinds of conversations are they having?

It is not surprising to notice that there are impressive differences between the way physicians communicate on medical social networks and on consumer social networks (i.e. Facebook, Twitter, etc.). Recent studies show that Twitter is used by doctors to primarily share news and third-party content (e.g. medical information, latest trial results, medical education, etc.), while conversations on medical social networks include storytelling and sharing personal experiences. Consumer social platforms are used to a much lesser extent than medical social platforms to discuss medicine and engage with other doctors.

The recent digital revolution in healthcare and the changing role of physicians make this difference even bigger. Doctors need a place to connect, share and be listened safely to safeguard themselves from both liability and privacy risks. Indeed, most doctors don't engage professionally on consumer social networks where they are identifiable. Rather, they prefer medical networks, where they can remain anonymous and feel free to express themselves genuinely.

As a consequence, listening to medical social platforms (i.e. Sermo, Doximity, DailyRounds, etc.) is critical to have a clear understanding of their needs, wants and limitations.

As you may easily understand, listening to the physicians' needs and wants is no longer a passive activity nowadays. As they take advantage of medical social platforms to instantly and publicly express their opinions, experiences and reactions, they expect faster responsiveness from healthcare organizations. Consequently, while you are listening it is critical to promptly and effectively manage the online discussion and most importantly take proper actions and or use their insights to develop tools capable of meeting their medical and clinical care priorities. We'll read more about this in Chapter 4.

Given the increasing number of physicians and patients using the Internet to voice their needs and/or complaints, that is, chat rooms, complaint-specific websites and disease-related message boards, blogs, forums, crowdsourcing communities, etc., genuinely concerned organizations should at the very least devise technology to "listen" to the chatter that goes on outside of their corporate website.

A successful organization should equip itself with a "social media command center" to monitor Internet activity for customer chatter and questions, while assisting those who need feedback or guidance live, and as it happens (i.e. chat bot).

A properly trained staff taking a similar approach for any organization working in the health industry (that is, pharma, HCPs, and so on) would go a long way to bridging the gap between industry and end-user.

Pysician needs, wants, and limitations

Based on a new survey which builds on a 2016 American Medical Association (AMA) survey of 1,300 physicians and aims to deepen the understanding of why doctors do or don't adopt new digital health solutions[4] physicians have concerns about technology's efficacy and evidence base, are apprehensive about IT's impact on payment, liability and quality of care, and are eager for solutions that give them back more face-to-face time with patients.

One of the key questions physicians make about digital health is "Does it work in my practice?"

To explore this question and explore how the technology will work in a physician's practice, the "Physician Adoption of Digital Health Technology" study was conducted by researchers at the AMA in collaboration with Partners HealthCare. The collaborative research team was led by principal investigator Kamal Jethwani, MD, MPH, senior director of Connected Health Innovation at Partners HealthCare, and co-investigator Dr. Kirley.

"What we started seeing is even though we had over 3,000 papers, not many of them actually talked about provider adoption. They weren't studying it, they weren't talking about it and they weren't mentioning it," Dr. Jethwani said. "We actually ended up with only 57 studies with any mention of provider adoption." Among the included studies, more than half (56 percent) of the digital health solutions had been implemented in primary care settings, while 19 percent were in specialty settings and 25 percent in both. Researchers determined that outcomes results were needed for patients and physicians. "That interplay is very important. If you have a lot of unengaged patients, the provider is going to lose interest," Dr. Jethwani said. "If you have an unengaged provider, the patients lose interest after a point."

While the information provided at the Connected Health Conference was not final, the interim results showed key facilitators of adoption for physicians included:

- the availability of additional resources and training;
- access to accurate data;
- positive impact on quality of care;
- evidence base for the digital health solution.

For this and a number of other similar studies, we can easily state that the main need for physicians to adopt a digital health solution is to feel very comfortable with the idea that this solution, providing evidence and demonstrating that it's going to help them take better care of their patients.

In addition, when looking at physician feedback, Dr. Kirley, member of the research team, shared one physician's response, "We need to know that the *data* is accurate and reliable to take action based on it." Another major need for physicians is that digital health solutions be designed in a way that they take them away from their screen and give them back to their patients.

"A lot of themes are common between patients and providers," said Dr. Jethwani. "As innovators and startup company executives, this makes your life easier because if you address the same exact issue, it is going to help on both sides of the aisle."

"If we are able to solve the system issue using digital health, then the patient-provider relationship can improve drastically because now you're actually creating a meaningful relationship," he added.

To ensure new digital health solutions facilitate effective care and relationships between patients and physicians, the AMA brings the physician voice to innovators and entrepreneurs. By recognizing the key challenges physicians face when implementing health IT and the increase of direct-to-consumer digital health apps, the AMA aims to help physicians navigate and maximize technology for improved patient care and professional satisfaction.

Delivering experiences is key to digital tools adoption

As highlighted in Chapter 2, experience is what drives digital tools' adoption for both physicians and patients, so in order for your physicians and patients to become adopters as long as advocates you need to deliver them that experience not only through your devices but also through effective and valuable services, communication tools and contents.

In a *Harvard Business Review* blog,[5] a survey of social media users suggested that speed of response was critical to "social support" success and that the user expectation is to see a response within hours. The article does go on to say that 30% of social media users surveyed prefer this technology to using the phone. The financial benefits are clear also, with the study citing a social support interaction costing less than $1, compared to email ($2.50–$5.00) and telephone ($6).

As an example,[6] patients familiar with technology at a Sutton Coldfield hospital can give feedback on their treatment and stay via smartphone. The Heart of England NHS Foundation which runs Good Hope Hospital in Sutton Coldfield has released a new Heart of England NHS Foundation Trust (HEFT) Patient Feedback app for Apple iPhones and an Android app available via the Google Play store. The free app is designed to create a communication channel between patients and the hospital to promptly give their thoughts on visiting an area of the hospital or staying on a ward. They can rate the ward on their experience, offer their thoughts and suggestions, and even get in touch with Trust Board members. The message, which is anonymous, will be addressed and responded to within 48 hours as part of the hospital's commitment to openness and transparency. The response will then appear within the app.

As experiences with digital tools are key to their effective adoption it is critical to understand the entire physician-and-patient journey. As anticipated, toward this aim, *experience mapping* can be a very useful tool to help hospitals and pharma/ biomedical/life sciences organizations find out what physicians and patients really think and feel about their clinical and healthcare experience respectively. The concept of *experience mapping* was first introduced by website developers to determine online users' experience as they moved from page to page. It is different from process mapping and traditional patient satisfaction research, which help organizations understand the customer experience at each step in the process from beginning to end. Experience mapping helps develop a strong customer-centric focus. It is a strategic change in focus from operations to customer. It explains the emotions behind the actions. It is most valuable when customer relationships are complex and involve multiple "touch points" or points of contact—perfect for hospitals or health management for drugs/biomedical products/devices.

More specifically, it is an in-depth qualitative research technique utilizing a visual cue (The Experience Map) to help patients, their family members, and their referring physicians recall specific episodes in their journey. Many studies show that direct and actual physician-and-patient feedback provide the best insights into understanding, improving, and managing the experience. Experience mapping enables organizations to evaluate the most important touch points, functional needs and emotional needs at each step of the journey.[7]

The main actions involved in experience mapping (Experience Mapping Process) are:

- identify the key steps before, during, and after a patient visits the facility;
- determine the activities patients and families go through at each step;
- assess which type of touch point delivers the brand's promise for each activity;
- talk to patients and families about their functional and emotional needs at each step;
- consolidate the findings into a "Voice of the Customer" report;
- determine the priorities of touch points and performance of each;
- identify key opportunities for improvement in care, coordination and communication;
- review patient stories to identify candidates for testimonials;
- develop meaningful messages by understanding attitudes, differentiators and reasons to believe.

Design and test physician/patient-driven digital tools and technology

Once healthcare managers and designers fully understand physicians and patients, they can design physician-and-patient-driven digital tools.

Participatory design

Participatory design approaches, such as "design thinking" and "maker movement," involving physicians, patients and caregivers, have the potential to create innovative and disruptive health solutions that improve care experiences for everyone.

Participatory Design (PD) is a further development of action research.[8] Action research involves collaboration between researchers and participants, and is a relatively new practice.[9] Participation is essential in PD research.[10] User participation in healthcare planning is important, especially when developing new healthcare technologies.[11,12] When users have participated in the development of new technologies, the chances of successful implementation in clinical practice are increased.

Participatory design is a product design method to design digital services. It involves stakeholders, end-users and the team in the design process in order to help ensure that the end-product meets the needs of users. As participatory design and all collaborative practices aim to respond better to needs of users, it could be considered as an approach more focused on processes and procedures of design and not the design (result) itself.

As an example, serious digital games can be effective at changing healthy lifestyles, but large differences in their effectiveness exist. The extent of user-involvement in game design may contribute to game effectiveness by creating a better fit with user preferences. Participatory design, which represents active user-involvement as informant (i.e. users are asked for input and feedback) or codesigner (i.e., users as equal partners in the design) early on and throughout the game development, may be associated with higher game effectiveness, as opposed to no user-involvement or limited user-involvement.[13]

A number of methods have shown to be effective in providing valuable insights for digital tools design. These include:

- *Co-designing with your users*: users can be involved at various stages of your product creation. Whether to test your product or to co-design it, users' thoughts and interventions should be carefully planned for specific stages in order to be effective.
- *Co-designing with your team*: it might start with an informal chat or if a detailed session is preferred, workshops can be a better start. A workshop session can be used to brainstorm or get various points of view about the product. You can start a co-designing workshop with your team to get various wireframes of the same screen. It encourage interactions and critics between participants and get people engaged on the whole design process.

Human-centered design

IDEO is one of the most innovative and award-winning design firms in the world. They're like the secret weapon of innovation for companies like Microsoft, Hewlett-Packard, Pepsi and Samsung. Over the last few decades, they've designed hundreds of products, like the first computer mouse for Apple in 1980, the Palm Pilot in 1998, a school system in Peru, and the 25-foot mechanical whale used in the movie *Free Willy*—to name a few.[14]

IDEO's main tenet is empathy for the end-user of their products. They believe that the key to figuring out what humans *really want* lies in doing two things:

- *Observing user behavior*—Try to understand people through observing them. For example, if you're designing a vacuum cleaner, watch people vacuum.
- *Putting yourself in the situation of the end-user*—IDEO does this to understand what the user experience is really like; to feel what their users feel.

Then, they use the information they gain to fuel their designs.

IDEO designers trust that, as long as they stay connected to the behaviors and needs of the people they're designing for, their ideas will evolve into the right solution. In other words, they let the end-user tell them what they need to focus on building.

"If you want to improve a piece of software all you have to do is watch people using it and see when they grimace, and then you can fix that," says David Kelley, Founder of IDEO.

Sometimes the best ideas are so obviously staring us in the face that we miss them. We can't see them because we're looking at things from the outside in, instead of looking at things through the eyes of the end-user. That's why the folks at IDEO strategically put users at the core of everything they do—a process they refer to as human-centered design.

IDEO defines human-centered design as a creative approach to problem solving that starts with people and ends with innovative solutions that are tailor made to suit their needs.

In their Field Guide to Human-Centered Design they say, "When you understand the people you're trying to reach—and then design from their perspective—not only will you arrive at unexpected answers, but you'll come up with ideas that they'll embrace."

This is the central philosophy that human-centered design revolves around. Whether you're designing physical or digital solutions, the process is the same and it consists of *six phases*:

Phase 1: Observation

The first phase is all about observing the end-user, learning, and being open to creative possibilities.

Your goal is to understand the people you're designing for.

Identify patterns of behavior, pain points and places where users have a difficult time doing something—these all lend to tremendous opportunity. If you can, put yourself in their situation so you can see what their experience is, and feel what they feel.

Phase 2: Ideation

In this phase you start brainstorming ideas with your team (Figure 3.3) based on what you learned from your observations and experiences in Phase 1.

Your goal is to come up with as many ideas as you can.

Figure 3.3 Brainstorming
Image courtesy of IDEO

Figure 3.4 Prototyping
Image courtesy of IDEO

As you're coming up with ideas, stay focused on the needs and desires of the people you're designing for. If you do this, your group's ideas will eventually evolve into the right solution.

Phase 3: Rapid prototyping

In this phase you're going to quickly build a simple prototype of your idea (Figure 3.4). This makes it tangible and gives you something to test with the end-user.

Don't try to build a fancy high-fidelity prototype right now. IDEO is notorious for creating simple prototypes made out of cardboard.

Ask yourself this: What can I spend the minimum amount of time building that will allow me to get user feedback as quickly as possible? The purpose of this phase isn't to create the perfect solution, it's to make sure your solution is on target.

Phase 4: User feedback

Get your simple prototype into the hands of the people you're designing for.

This is the most critical phase of the human-centered design process. Without input from your end-user you won't know if your solution is on target or not, and you won't know how to evolve your design.

Phase 5: Iteration

Once you get feedback from your users, use that information to fuel the changes to your design.

Keep iterating, testing, and integrating user feedback until you've fine-tuned your solution. This may take a few rounds, but don't get discouraged. With each iteration you'll learn something new.

Once you've got your solution to a point where it's ready to be used, it's time to move on to the next and final phase.

Phase 6: Implementation

Now that you've validated the usefulness of your solution with the end-user and got your design just right, it's time to get your idea out into the world.

If you're designing software products, apps or websites, go back to Phase 1 and repeat this process. With each new update that you implement, continue to observe your users, design for them, and use their feedback to direct your future solutions.

Examples of human-centered design at IDEO

IDEO has used this process over and over again to design delightful products and experiences that people love.

You might be wondering how exactly you're supposed to get started. How do you start observing your users? How do you put yourself in their position?

Let's take a look at a few examples that illustrate IDEO's human-centered design process so you can apply it to your own team.

Example #1: Designing a medical device for nurses

IDEO was asked by a medical device producer to design a device that nurses would use to enter data during a specific procedure. The client had a vision of a sleek, futuristic gadget that the nurses would hold with two hands (picture how someone would hold an iPad) during the operation.

But when the IDEO team watched the medical procedure take place, they noticed something that would make a two-handed device completely impossible.

When patients were going into the operation they were really nervous and afraid. So the first thing that almost every nurse did was hold the patient's hand to comfort them—an obvious human element their client hadn't noticed.

IDEO went back to their office to brainstorm potential solutions, and they came up with a device that had a thumb scroll so nurses could do everything with one hand. That way they could input data and hold the patient's hand.

It wasn't as "cool" as the client initially imagined, but it was much more human and practical.

Instead of approaching the project with preconceived notions of what the solution needed to be, the IDEO team started by putting themselves in the position of the end-user.

Then they used that information to direct their ideas, and even though they ended up designing something that was different than what they initially expected, they created a much more human experience for everybody involved.

Example #2: Improving a hospital's patient experience

IDEO was asked by a large healthcare system to describe what their patient experience was like, and to help them improve it.

So the IDEO team started by putting themselves in the position of the patient. They had one of their team members pretend to be a patient in the hospital, and they discovered something obvious, yet completely overlooked.

When they presented their findings to the hospital executives, they started by showing a six-minute video clip of the ceiling in a patient's room. At first the executives were confused and didn't understand what they were watching. Then the IDEO team explained the purpose of the video.

The point was this: when you're a patient in the hospital you spend all day lying in a bed staring at the ceiling for a really long time—and it's a really bad experience.

Watching that video clip helped the executives catch what IDEO's Chief Creative Officer Paul Bennett calls "a blinding glimpse of the bloody obvious."

Looking at the patient experience from the point of view of the patient—instead of the organization—was a huge revelation to them, and they immediately took action. They realized that improving the patient experience wasn't about making massive changes to the system. Instead, it's about doing small things that make a big impact.

So IDEO started brainstorming ideas and prototyping, and they quickly implemented small four changes:

1. Decorated the ceilings to make them more aesthetically pleasing.
2. Covered one wall of each patient's room with whiteboards so visitors could write messages for the patient.
3. Made the floor of patient rooms a different style and color than the floor in the hallways of the hospital. This signified the transition from public space to private space, making patients feel like this was their own personal space.
4. Attached rear-view mirrors to hospital gurneys, so that when patients were wheeled around by a doctor or nurse they could actually see the person they were having a conversation with.

There's a long history of innovative designers observing the world around them, seeing things with a fresh eye, and using that observation as an opportunity to create new possibilities. The common thread that ties all these stories together is a design process that starts with understanding the end-user of your product.

IDEO does this by observing the user, and putting themselves in the user's shoes. They know that if they can feel what people feel—what their experience is really like—then they can use that information to fuel their design solutions. To build a truly innovative and useful product, you don't need to start with the brightest idea or the fanciest technology. You just need to start by understanding people.

Design a physician-and-patient-driven adoption strategy

As we have already seen, based on recent studies, a number of barriers and facilitators to the adoption of e-health technology by physicians can be identified. Technology represents advances in knowledge that change the way humans perform tasks. Ideally, technology will make the task easier, more efficient, safer or perhaps more pleasurable. Unfortunately, new technologies can sometimes make a task more difficult, slower, dangerous or perhaps more frustrating. If we consider for example older adults, they interact with a variety of technologies in the course of their daily activities and thus products should be designed to be used by people of varying ages.

In Chapter 6, dedicated to digital tools adoption and diffusion, we provide an overview of what psychology has to offer to the design of technology—from understanding what people need, to identifying their preferences for design characteristics, and to defining their capabilities and limitations that will influence technology interactions.

Rogers' four main elements that influence the spread of new ideas (innovation, communication channels, time and a social system) rely heavily on human capital. The ideas must be widely accepted in order to be self-sustainable. Designers must consider various cultures and communities to predict how, why and at what rate new ideas and technology will be adopted.

By categorizing consumers, the designer can identify particular segments with a market sector to gain feedback. By engaging with these stereotypes, the designer can utilize their experiences with a prototype in order to guide further development.

Preparing an integrated marketing communication plan

The organization's digital strategy outlines which customers (i.e. physicians, patients, other stakeholders) it will target and how it will create value for them.

Once all the physician-and-patient touch points are clear you will need to design an integrated communication plan that includes both online and offline tactics/tools to communicate and promote internally and externally the effective use of the new digital tools.

The first step to integration is to analyze your existing set of tools and channels (that is, website, blog, email newsletter(s), paper magazine or newsletter, direct mailing, Facebook, Twitter, YouTube).

Having an effective integrated communication strategy requires that you understand how each type of media relates to the other and that you have a program that ensures they strengthen and complement each other to generate patient value.

In order to avoid the "using everything" mistake, it is important to have a clear understanding of the strengths and distinctive features of each channel before getting too far trying to integrate different communication channels you need.

Planning is crucial to integration. Step back and look at each year as a whole. What are the big events that will shape your communication? Is there an awareness week or other national campaign you usually get involved in?

Last but not least, ensure that you are tracking your progress.

Tracking progress not only justifies all of your work to others but it also helps keep you motivated and focused on strategic goals. You should tailor your key performance indicators (KPIs) to your organization, but it is recommended that you review them on a monthly basis, ideally with a wider team in the organization.

Building valuable relationships and collaboration

The first five steps in the digital communication process—understanding what physicians' and patients' needs and wants are; designing physician-and-patient-driven digital tools; testing digital tools design, technology and clinical evidence; designing a physician-and-patient-driven adoption strategy; and constructing an integrated communication program—all lead up to the sixth and most important step: building and managing valuable relationships.

Provider–patient relationship

The relationship between provider and patient forms the foundation of healthcare and is vitally important to both parties. It is the vehicle for sharing information, feelings and concerns; a crucial factor in the success of treatment; and an essential component in the satisfaction of both patient and practitioner.[15]

Nevertheless, cost-containment efforts, pressures for higher productivity, a managerial rather than professional perspective on healthcare, and increased dependence on technology all have the potential to prevent the capacity of practitioners to develop and demonstrate effective, caring relationships with their patients.

In recent years, effective communication has been found to produce better health outcomes, a greater probability that patients will follow recommendations, and a reduced risk of malpractice suits. These are particularly significant considering the increasing emphasis in the contemporary healthcare system on improving quality and outcomes, increasing patient satisfaction and reducing or containing costs.

Some basic strategies useful to create effective online relationships are:[16]

- Offer information that is relevant and valuable for the patients. Though this may sound easy, most of the HCP websites today miss this key point. They provide a lot of information, often even too much—but little of what consumers consider to be valued.

- Pay attention to designing and offering patient-care key services. A valuable web strategy starts by providing complete information, including online experience tools, about the key services the HCP provides.
- Be consistent and provide the promised online services. Different to print media and television, websites can truly and effectively provide services.
- Involve nurses, clinicians and any other caregivers who bring the patients in the website. An HCP's website will be of little value if it neglects the input, awareness and ownership of physicians and other clinicians. In fact, the best way to attract qualified users (a local person dealing with a medical or health problem) is to make sure that physicians and other caregivers have been actively involved in the development of the information on the site so that they can advocate it to their patients.
- Start an online relationship with a "signal event." A "signal event" happens when a patient is initially being informed about a health condition that is possibly going to change his/her life. Regardless of it being positive (a woman learns that she is pregnant) or negative (a man learns he has cancer) the person involved will be highly motivated to seek information concerning the medical condition and its treatment options.
- Use a "clicks and mortar" approach to your web services. A website's design and content should be designed with the aim of turning health information seekers into service users in case of need.

Industry–patient relationship

Companies marketing drugs and medical devices very often talk the language of patient-centricity but rarely do they concretely and effectively provide it. Constrained by regulations in many countries limiting what can, and cannot, be communicated to patients or divulged to the public, industry has battled for years to obtain more openness with regulatory regimes that actively limit its possibility to communicate with end-user customers.

Whatever industry does, it will have to face the concern that when profit is part of the health equation, then its motives can be questioned. The funding of patient groups and related patient-focused initiatives leaves the industry open to the accusation that, by encouraging actions and patient pressure on health payers and Health Technology Assessment bodies, it can achieve what it is unable to do through normal regulatory channels: advance reimbursement and product use while driving sales.

With the increasing use of the Internet and social media, though, demand for information and dialog is developing rapidly. The industry's response—whether by choice or regulatory burden—has not yet been effective and completely fulfilling. If the common aims of patients and industry are to be really reciprocally valuable, the industry has to raise its patient–relations game.

Partner relationship management

When it comes to creating customer value and building strong customer relationships, today's health communicators know that they cannot go it alone. They must work closely with a variety of communication partners. In addition to being good at customer relationship management, health communicators must also be good at partner relationship management—working closely with others inside and outside the organization to jointly bring more value to customers.

In today's more connected world, every functional area in the organization can interact with patients. The new accepted wisdom is that—no matter what your job is in a company—you must understand marketing and be patient-focused. Rather than letting each division go its own way, organizations must link all divisions in the cause of creating value. Health communicators must also partner with institutions, patient, and physician associations.

Building productive relationships in the healthcare industry

At the basis of effective provider–patient/industry–patient relationships lies productive relationships in the industry as a whole. Indeed, though very important in any organization, productive ongoing relationships are often critical in the healthcare industry and even more when dealing with digital communication. In fact, not only can poor relationships and conflict lead to patient suffering or harm, they can also ignite collaborative care-giving which characterizes these types of organizations.

Although we know that relationships are often demanding, especially in high workload or pressure situations, such as healthcare, the fact is that as individuals and organizations we typically take relationships for granted. As a consequence, sooner or later, many of our working relationships need maintenance. They need us to get the right skills to make them work effectively. They need a willingness to adapt, to listen to others, to accept different perspectives and approaches. A good way to think about this is in terms of more relationship "enabling" behavior and less "challenging" behavior as shown in the Table 3.1.[17]

Table 3.1 Relationship analysis grid

Enablers	(need more of) listening, patience, clear communication, honest/open communication, cooperation, teamwork
Challengers	(need less of) personal agendas, ego, over-communication, stress, interpersonal conflict, lack of clarity, ambiguity
Sustainers	(create and maintain) openness, assertiveness, effective conflict handling skills, good feedback processes

Using this grid can help to quickly turn the situation around in any health-care organization, even where the current culture is difficult, or relationships are severely strained at individual or functional level (nurses and doctors having ongoing conflict issues for example). The secret is to begin in one area (probably where the problems are at their worst) and use the new behaviors learned to apply more extensively while trust about what works best starts to increase.

Capturing value from empowered patients

The final step of the digital strategy process outlined in Figure 1.3 involves capturing value in return in the form of effective patient empowerment, positive health behavior, healthcare outcomes, and profits. Government, pharmaceutical companies and managed care alike have a shared goal of helping people live longer and more productive lives. They differ on how to get there; however, there is a shared consensus that improving health can deliver significant economic benefits to society. Empowered patients represent an important asset for government, pharmaceutical companies and managed care alike.

The need for strategic alignment

In my research and consultancy with companies, I observe that often no individual or group is functionally responsible for overseeing the arrangement of their company from end to end. Multiple different individuals and groups are responsible for different components of the value chain that make up their company's design, and they are often not as joined up as they should be. All too often, individual leaders seek—indeed are incentivized—to protect and optimize their own domains, and find themselves locked in energy-sapping internal turf wars, rather than working with peers to align and improve across the entire enterprise. Achieving sustainable competitive advantage through superior strategic alignment does not happen by accident—it happens by design, or not at all, and it requires a special breed of leadership, which Jonathan Trevor calls enterprise leadership.[18]

"A shared strategy and its effective execution is critical to successful physician and patient empowerment with digital tools."

Notes

1 Ramez Shehadi et al. (2012), "IT and healthcare: Evolving together at the Cleveland Clinic." *strategy+business magazine*, published by Booz & Company Inc. [online]. Available at http://case.edu/newmeded/downloads/it-and-healthcare.pdf [Accessed February 12, 2018].
2 Eric Almquist (2016), "The 30 things customers really value." *Harvard Business Review*.
3 Letizia Affinito and John Mark (2015), *Socialize Your Patient Engagement Strategy: How Social Media and Mobile Apps Can Boost Health Outcomes*. Abingdon: Routledge.
4 Sara Berg (2018), "These factors interfere with physicians' IT adoption." *American Medical Association*. [online]. Available at https://wire.ama-assn.org/practice-management/these-factors-interfere-physicians-it-adoption [Accessed February 19, 2018].
5 G. Benmark and D. Singer (2012), "Turn customer care into 'Social care' to break away from the competition." HBR Blog Network [online]. Available at http://blogs.hbr.org/cs/2012/12/turn_customer_care_into_social.html [Accessed September 30, 2014].
6 N. Horner (2013). [online]. Available at www.lichfieldmercury.co.uk/Patient-engagement-makes-smart/story-20232218-detail/story.html [Accessed December 13, 2014].
7 Gelb Consulting Group, Inc. (2014), "Using experience mapping to build patient enchantment." This article originally appeared in *Healthcare Strategy Alert! Forum for Healthcare Strategists*.
8 K. Garne Holm, A. Brødsgaard, G. Zachariassen, A.C. Smith and J. Clemensen (2017), "Participatory design methods for the development of a clinical telehealth service for neonatal homecare." *SAGE Open Medicine*, 5, 2050312117731252. http://doi.org/10.1177/2050312117731252. [online]. Available at https://www.ncbi.nlm.nih.gov/pmc/articles/PMC5613838/. [Accessed March 9, 2018].
9 J. Clemensen, M.J. Rothmann, A.C. Smith, L.J. Caffery and D.B. Danbjorg (2017), "Participatory design methods in telemedicine research." *J Telemed Telecare*, 23(9), 780–785. [PubMed].
10 J.R.T. Simonsen (2013), *Routledge International Handbook of Participatory Design*. New York: Routledge, p. 295.
11 J.R.T. Simonsen (2013), *Routledge International Handbook of Participatory Design*. New York: Routledge, p. 295.
12 M. Kyng (1998), "Users and computers: A contextual approach to design computer artefacts." *Scan J Inform Syst*, 10, 7–44.
13 A. DeSmet, D. Thompson, T. Baranowski, A. Palmeira, M. Verloigne and I. De Bourdeaudhuij (2016), "Is participatory design associated with the effectiveness of serious digital games for healthy lifestyle promotion? A meta-analysis." *J Med Internet Res*, 18(4), e94 doi:10.2196/jmir.4444 PMID: 27129447 PMCID: 4867751. [online]. Available at www.jmir.org/2016/4/e94/n [Accessed March 9, 2018].
14 UserTesting (2015), "IDEO's 6 step human-centered design process: How to make things people want." [online]. Available at https://www.usertesting.com/blog/2015/07/09/

how-ideo-uses-customer-insights-to-design-innovative-products-users-love/ [Accessed March 9, 2018].

15 Letizia Affinito and John Mark (2015), *Socialize Your Patient Engagement Strategy: How Social Media and Mobile Apps Can Boost Health Outcomes.* Abingdon: Routledge.

16 C.L. Thomas (2002), "Seven strategies for building effective online relationships." *Health Progress*, pp. 9, 56 [online]. Available at https://www.chausa.org/docs/default-source/health-progress/net-gains---seven-strategies-for-building-effective-online-relationships-pdf.pdf?sfvrsn=0 [Accessed December 15, 2014].

17 J. Warner (2013), *Building Productive Relationships in the Healthcare Industry: Climate and Culture.* [online]. Available at http://blog.readytomanage.com/building-productive-relationships-in-the-healthcare-industry/. [Accessed December 15, 2014].

18 Jonathan Trevor (2018), "Is anyone in your company paying attention to strategic alignment?" *Harvard Business Review.* [online]. Availble at https://hbr.org/2018/01/is-anyone-in-your-company-paying-attention-to-strategic-alignment [Accessed March 9, 2018].

Listening to physicians **4**

How behavioral analytics and social media fuel more personalized communication (online market research and web listening)

In the first step of the Digital Health Strategy Process Model (Figure 1.3), healthcare organizations work to understand physicians and patient needs, wants and limitations. The Internet offers the opportunity to do this and also engage with physicians and patients' communities. Listening and engaging must be an iterative process which never stops. This is how you build great customer experiences.

In this chapter we will explore the definitions of passive and active listening and see how passive listening can be far more action-oriented and intent-filled than it sounds. Both types of listening can lead to a lot of action; after all, isn't that the point of listening? We'll present the type of analysis you need for leverage and possible applications for both passive and active listening. Finally, we will explore how managers gain insights into patients' needs and how companies develop and manage information about important health system elements: physicians, patients, competitors, producers and other relevant stakeholders. To succeed in today's health system companies and organizations must know how to turn mountains of information into fresh customer insights that will help them deliver greater value to customers.

We'll start with a **leading case history** about listening and engaging in action at the American Medical Association (AMA), which, recognizing the importance of physicians providing feedback to health tech entrepreneurs for improved solutions, has developed a beta version of the AMA Physician Innovation Network—a platform to connect and match physicians and the health tech community. The Physician Innovation Network is an online networking site that connects and matches physicians and health tech entrepreneurs/companies to collaborate in developing improved solutions in healthcare. The goal of the platform is multi-faceted. For physicians, it presents an opportunity to examine paid and volunteer ways to work with up-and-coming healthcare companies. It also gives health tech start-ups a way to search for specific doctors who would be able to provide feedback on their products and services. Additionally, the platform gives both parties a chance to share innovative ideas and access expert insight via online panel discussions.

AMA and non-AMA members are able to join the platform, which is currently of no cost to physicians and entrepreneurs.

Passive and active listening

There are essentially two types of listening to social media: active and passive. The distinction is very important because it potentially involves using different strategies and tools.

Let's start by clarifying what listening means in this context. It could be defined as observing content generated by all users of social media (that is, Facebook, Google Plus Hangouts, TweetChats, LinkedIn Groups, medical networks) including private citizens, the private sector, nongovernmental organizations, and all levels of governmental—local, state and federal. Active listening includes all of the above with the added element of interaction.[1]

While managers have exercised active and passive forms of listening in the past, social media has made both versions more valuable. In fact, social media provides several unique benefits to the practice of listening—especially as it relates to customers.

During passive listening—sometimes called monitoring—a business attempts to understand what is being discussed in the marketplace as though the business were a fly on the wall. It acts as a spectator and remains uninvolved, until and only if direct attention is needed.

Social media has drastically augmented the value of passive listening in two respects. First, passive access to conversations in social media is immediate, digital, and worldwide. Quiet proximity to the discussions is ubiquitous, and the digital chatter becomes manageable, filterable insightful content, assuming the proper tools are in place to hear a mention of your brand/ initiative/organization/service on all relevant social platforms, blogs, ratings and review sites where these conversations land. Second, passive listeners monitoring social media can engage a customer in need, to address dissatisfactions or to tactfully offer tips to those seeking advice.

Consider this scenario. A patient keeps calling his/her physician asking for help with his/her brand new compliance app. Both physician and patient are getting frustrated about it because it is impacting the treatment efficacy. One day, frustrated enough, the patient tweets with dismay: "Yuck. The new app from X company is worthless ... it is complicated to use and some options don't work properly and the treatment doesn't work. I'll ask the doctor for a new app!"

The patient's opinion is retweeted across their network. A close friend posts the rant to Facebook. Left unheard and unaddressed, the digital reach of this "did-you-hear" beacon can accelerate across the 40 to 50 top ratings and review sites and blogs. Same destiny will have the physician's opinion posted in twitter while a different destiny it will have in a leading medical network (i.e. Sermo) where the physician's opinion will still be shared among all the community members with a more limited audience impact.

Unless someone from the organization or a trained doctor/nurse was there to ask if everything was OK, the traditional form of passive listening fails here.

Successful organizations have a solution that tells physicians and patients exactly how to fix that problem. Listening gives leading organizations the opportunity to learn about the problem and proactively deliver that solution on YouTube and point folks to that.

It is now possible—indeed advisable—for companies committed to developing and introducing innovative health digital tools to pay attention to what and how it is being discussed online.

The trick here is twofold: have the tools in place to listen to all possible social platforms, and most important, understand how and when to tactfully engage and appease that once loyal customer.

In contrast to passive listening, active listening is an engaged approach wherein a business proactively creates an opportunity for a customer to give them feedback—usually with the intention of using that feedback to drive an action. With active listening, you pull responses back to you in order to capture value from customers, physicians or patients (see Figure 1.3 in Chapter 3).

Perhaps one of the most outstanding examples of active web listening is represented by the Domino's striking "Pizza Turnaround" campaign.[2]

After five years of sluggish or decreasing revenues, Domino's Pizza made a remarkable revolution in its industry, and one that all B2B or B2C organizations, even from the healthcare industry, can learn from.

First, it invited customers to give their sincere opinion. Second, it truly listened to the burning truth about their product (that is, "cardboard crust" and "totally devoid of flavor"). Finally the company reinvented its product "from the crust up." The *turnaround* began with marketing research to become aware of what customers felt and wanted. To acquire further insights into what customers really felt about its pizzas, Domino's decided to start online marketing research. It listened to consumers' online chats and prompted thousands of direct consumer feedback messages via Facebook, Twitter, and other social media. Using the insights gained online, it started a series of old-fashioned, well-established focus groups to involve customers in face-to-face conversations. Rather than covering up the burning results or flaunting them off, Domino's management recognized the problems and tried to solve them. Domino's began by totally reinventing its pizzas. To communicate the changes and to change customer opinions, Domino's launched a $75 million "Pizza Turnaround" promotion campaign: the research itself was the message. The surprisingly straightforward campaign was entirely integrated into the brand's Facebook and Twitter pages, where the company posted both the bad and the good and asked for continuing opinion and advice. The entire *turnaround* story—from biting focus group footage to the shocked reactions of Domino's executives and hard work to reinvent the product—was edited in a forthright four-and-half minute behind-the-scenes documentary which was published on the website www.pizzaturnaround.com visible for all to see. The campaign was risky but, considering the results, the straightforward approach worked. The transparent ads and message seized consumer interest and changed opinions. The message for marketers from any industry is that having a constructive conversation with customers, listening to their opinions, and, most of all, effectively using the resulting insights can generate significant outcomes.

If the fundamental goal of any organization providing products and services in the healthcare industry is to fulfill the needs of its patients then it is critically important to listen to them and understand their needs. When you get to know physicians and patients' needs, you have higher and better chances to include valuable tools and tactics in your digital strategy and so provide value for your physician and customer or patient while, at the same time, boosting profits for your organization.

Social media has created more valuable forms of both passive and active listening, resulting in a better understanding of the physician and patient. Find out what your physicians and patients need, give it to them, and bring in the rewards. It starts with listening.

How to choose the right social media monitoring tool? If a social analytics solution for market research does not offer all of the following features you should probably walk away and look for one that does (DigitalMR, a

London-headquartered technology company in the market research sector with proprietary technology for online communities and social media listening):[3]

1. A clear and easy way to get rid of all the irrelevant posts—80% of the data you harvest could be noise.
2. Sentiment analysis in any language with the same accuracy—at least over 75%.
3. Semantic analysis in any language with the same accuracy—at least over 80%.
4. The ability to break down sentiment into specific emotions.
5. Image analysis for logo recognition and theme detection.
6. A clear process on how to integrate insights from social media listening with surveys and customer behavior tracking.

If you happen to be a customer insights practitioner and you are unhappy with the choice of social media monitoring tool your digital marketing department is using, because it does not seem to be addressing your own use cases, you have three options:

1. Accept that you will not be able to use social media listening to discover actionable insights—your organization will not be able to compete on the marketing place in the long run and you will probably be fired.
2. Argue a case to replace the tool that your colleagues in Digital are using with one that covers both your needs and theirs—this battle is very difficult to win because of the cost of switch as well as the "not invented here syndrome."
3. Argue a case that your organization needs an additional kind of a social listening tool with higher accuracy that will complement the one already in use by Digital—most likely scenario to succeed, especially if the tool used by digital marketing can be used for post harvesting and the social media research company will be happy to clean and analyze the data harvested by another tool.

How to integrate data from online surveys with social listening and analytics

Social listening and analytics have become an integral part of contemporary market research and discovering customer insights. Traditional research methods alone are no longer sufficient, nor fully representative, of how consumers perceive brands and products in today's business environment. Unless surveys are shorter, faster, and integrated with other sources of data such as social listening, they can no longer deliver the same value that they once did in the past.

In a recent article[4] Michalis Michael, DigitalMR (UK) and Divya Radhakrishnan, Nielsen (United Arab Emirates)(2017) aim to demonstrate how integrating social listening data with survey data, and other traditional research methods, can help companies uncover some of the most accurate insights possible. A case study revolving around Health & Wellness was selected as an example to illustrate the untapped power of social listening analytics.

Nielsen and DigitalMR have embarked on a long-term R&D project to determine the most effective methods to integrate consumer data from multiple sources in an impactful way for end-users of market research reports. The ultimate goal is to connect the dots and synthesize insights that were otherwise unattainable without integration (Michael, 2014).

There are only four different types of sources of information for the purpose of market research and customer insights (Michael, 2012):

- Asking questions (surveys and FGDs).
- Listening (from social media and other online sources, from call centers).
- Tracking behavior (loyalty card purchases, recorded transactions, Nielsen retail audits).
- Observing (ethnography, neuroscience).

As already stated, integrating these data sources can be considered as the "Holy Grail" of market research.

Online communities: public, gated or a hybrid?

Online communities, now a very popular means of interaction for people who know each other offline or have met online, can take a number of forms such as chat rooms, forums, video games, blogs and virtual worlds, email lists, or discussion boards. Online communities can "meet" around a common interest and can unfold across multiple websites.[5]

Once they have decided to go for an online community, organizations must decide which kind of community best meets its objectives: public, gated or a hybrid (largely public with a private, members-only area). Choosing one type of community over another will impact any single aspect of how it will work and, most of the times, even its success.

This fundamental decision depends basically on the characteristics of the audience the organization is planning to serve. For example, a public community is the right format to reach broad audiences. A private, gated community would probably work better to reach a small and focused audience. A hybrid format would better work in the case of multiple audience types or needs. Each type can have different benefits, risks and type of members (Table 4.1).[6]

Table 4.1 Main features to consider when choosing an online community

	Organization's Need	Members	Benefits	Risks
Public Online Communities	Engage a large audience of consumers or customers	Open to anyone on the web willing to join the conversation on a specific topic of interest	Wide reach, allows organizations to meet market penetration, product or service advocacy	Loss of brand or message control
Private Online Communities (POC) (Gated or invitation-only)	Create a sense of trust and intimacy among members Greater amount of insights about single members Shared acceptance criteria	Involves a highly targeted audience	Higher customer loyalty Higher client penetration of product and service purchases Better R&D and shorter time to market Get high-level expertise from members	Members expect higher levels of service Members selection criteria may limit final size High-quality content required Active community management required
Hybrid Online Communities (Both public and gated or private area within the whole community structure. Access determined by the members role. For example, an open, public area for patients with private, gated areas for HCPs and other medical professionals)	Need to serve a need or segment different from the one around which a public or private community has been developed and managed	Involves both a public (anyone) and a private (selective and targeted) membership	Market foresight Rewards of both having a private member-driven community and using very selective delivery of private content to attract a larger audience to the public space	

Setting up and managing a private online community

Private online communities (POCs) are dedicated, brand-sponsored platforms that allow the exchange of ideas and content via a suite of interactive features, like discussion forums, polls, libraries and member directories.

POCs can be categorized in three types:

- Innovation centers: set up to obtain in-depth interaction with customers and partners, these communities aim to share information, gather insights and act upon community-sourced ideas.
- Customer huggers: set up to support members needing assistance, they are short on deep interactions and collaboration with members. Consequently, valued insights stay unexplored.
- Marketing speakers: designed and managed most often to maximize Search Engine Optimization (SEO). These communities generate little interaction but aim to communicate a brand's attributes to potential and existing customers.
- Lead generators: set up by brands with the aim to involve members in conversations exclusively to generate sales leads. Whenever a potential customer joins the conversation the sales team jumps in to push the sale, stimulating neither confidence nor commitment.

Overall, successful online communities often bring together aspects of each of these four types, nevertheless, healthcare organizations must prioritize the first two styles (customer huggers and innovation centers) which offer brands the greatest potential to source content.

Online communities for engagement and community panels can be differentiated by the number of members they contain—ideally between 200–500 for co-creation and more than 1,000 members for community panels (Digital MR, 2012).[7] Large communities can also be used for quantitative online research in addition to using sub-communities for co-creation.

Owning the sample in a POC or community panel means that you only pay for sample acquisition and can then use it as and when required.

Panels and communities are quite distinct. Put simply, a panel is a group of consumers that a client will conduct surveys with—perhaps once a month or so. The client asks questions and panelists give their answers in a fairly structured way.

However, with a POC, not only can clients ask their community members questions using qualitative and quantitative research techniques, but also members can interact with the client (or host) and among themselves. The nature of the community allows them to do this in a much more unstructured and ad hoc way. Opening up these boundaries and restrictions posed by more conventional research enables communities to get you closer to your customers.

According to a social media study from Elsevier (2012),[8] online patient communities are not particularly popular among physicians. In fact, almost one-third of those interviewed thought they would be unlikely to ever use this form of social media.

One of the primary findings from the Elsevier study is that physicians seem to be more optimistic on using social media tools to interact with each other and that more than three-quarters of all physicians are likely to be involved in online physician communities over the coming five years. HCPs are currently using online physician communities (that is, SERMO) as a virtual form of "doctor's lounge," where they can discuss challenging patient issues with physicians who may have experienced similar concerns. These forms of social media offer instant contact for physicians to consult and exchange on current medical topics.

With regard to patient communities, the American Medical Association (AMA), based on reports by the PricewaterhouseCooper's Health Research Institute and from the Computer Sciences Corporation's (CSC) Global Institute for Emerging Healthcare Practices, identified that they are a good place for physicians to find out more information about topics patients are interested in, and thus what is important to their clients. In fact, opinions on social media sites about pharmaceuticals and therapies, healthcare services and experiences is a valued source of information. Furthermore, having instant access to a global community of peers easily available to consult with (that is, PatientsLikeMe) provides numerous and invaluable benefits.

Apparently the debate about whether the medical community is prepared to embrace social media as an important tool for sharing medical information and delivering high-quality care to patients is, basically, over.

The main focus will now be on identifying the most effective ways to support the practical use of physician and patient communities, guaranteeing the information provided is reliable and targeting the right audience.

One of the most excellent examples of POC development and management is at the basis of the online qualitative research launched by a healthcare foundation, the Crohn's and Colitis Foundation of Canada (CCFC) in order to shift its focus (Hancock, 2012).[9] For several years, in fact, the CCFC focused entirely on discovering a cure. Fundraising efforts to help fund research had always been a priority over disease education and patient assistance. Nevertheless, with an increasing number of patient requests for information and assistance, the Foundation sought to find the main patient needs and opportunities to differentiate. The qualitative research approach, developed, and implemented by the qualitative researcher Layla Shea, focused on making it easy for Crohn's and colitis patients to participate. She opted for an online method for two main reasons:

- Sensitivity to patient needs: Patients' difficulty to be away from home for even a few and social pressure resulting from discussing such a personal topic in a face-to-face setting.
- Geographic reach: Conducting online research allowed, in a single study, the involvement of respondents throughout the very large area served by CCFC. The research was planned to last ten days and included two activities each day:
  - *One poll*: the daily question "was today a good day or bad day and why?"
  - *One engagement activity*: Shea's activity-based conversations stimulated more discussion and personal interaction than a standard set of questions.

Activities aimed to allow participants to interact, share ideas and offer support. For example, the "Let's Vent" activity requested participants to post about their frustrations. They were encouraged to write about things that irritate them or post photos or videos that described how they felt. This activity generated a lively conversation among respondents, who instantly began building on each other's posts and stories.

Findings from the research helped identify three specific stages of Crohn's and colitis diagnoses and the needs associated with those stages:

1. Pre-diagnosis—"What's wrong with me?" The information needed while symptoms occur before a diagnosis is made.
2. At diagnosis—"Help me understand." The desire for more information about how the patient's life will be affected and what they need to manage the disease.
3. Post-diagnosis—"Help me take control." How can a patient create a meaningful life while managing this disease?

As a result, the CCFC created three specific communication strategies, tailoring tactics and messaging to the distinct needs and feelings of patients in each stage. In addition, it used the findings to realign its communication and education materials with the needs of both patients and HCPs.

The research truly helped the CCFC, which registered an increasing trend in the number of inquiries for information after the implementation of the new communication. There has also been a significant increase in the number of people attending CCFC conferences and educational events, as well as an increase in participation and donations at its fundraising events.

Even more importantly, the research is helping Crohn's and colitis patients satisfy their own specific needs and also benefit from the pleasure of helping others whose situations are similar to their own.

As the CCFC example shows, for a POC to develop into a long-term resource for an organization, it is crucial to get the right establishment and management of it.

Setting up and managing a POC from scratch can be an intimidating process, so it's suggested to break it down into the following stages (Digital MR, 2012):[10]

- Define the scope
  a) Size of the community
  b) Specific objectives and target members
  c) Customization

- Recruit members
  a) Use appropriate resources and channels to recruit members
  b) Appoint an Online Community Manager (OCM)

- Engage members
  a) Connect with members before starting activities
  b) Talk to members from the first day they join
  c) Connect them with each other
  d) Plan activities for the duration of the research

- Manage activities
  a) Execute research activities
  b) Encourage co-creation
  c) Reward participants when and how appropriate
  d) Share results

- Replenish members
  a) The OCM will minimize members attrition
  b) Some members will inevitably drop out
  c) Define a replenishment cycle

Main online physicians communities

A 2009 MDsearch survey[11] found that 72% of physicians are members of at least one social networking site. The past few years have introduced a number of online communities exclusively for physicians. They range from the truly exclusive sites like Sermo, an online community with an extensive credential verification process, to DocsBoard, an online forum requiring members to enter their license numbers, to sites like Tiromed, which asks registrants to affirm their physician or med student status on an honor system. Other sites such as MedScape and medXcentral are open to physicians as well as other healthcare professionals and do not require any proof of professional status. The growing list of online communities for physicians includes the following:

- *Clinical Village*—online network for medical community
- *DocnDoc*—online community for physicians
- *DocsBoard*—message boards for licensed physicians
- *Doctors Hangout*—online community for medical students, residents and physicians
- *DrConnected*—online network for physicians and healthcare professionals
- *iMedExhange*—online community for residents, physicians and retired physicians
- *Medical Passions*—online dating site for the medical community
- *MedScape*—online community for healthcare providers
- *MedicSpeak*—online community for medical students and physicians
- *medXcentral*—online community for all healthcare professionals, as well as healthcare recruiters
- *MomMD*—online community for women in medicine
- *New Media Medicine*—message boards for med school applicants, medical students and physicians
- *Ozmosis*—online community for licensed physicians only
- *Relax Doc*—online community for physicians only
- *Sermo*—online community for licensed physicians only
- *StudentDoc*—online community for medical students
- *Tiromed*—online community for physicians and students of medicine

Perhaps the most immediate benefit of these online medical communities is their capacity to facilitate instant "curbside consults" among physicians all over the country. Instead of a physician making a phone call to another physician for advice, doctors can turn to their online network and get real-time feedback from multiple physicians. In this way, online communities for physicians have a direct benefit to patients.

In addition, they provide a support system to busy physicians who don't have the time to attend conferences and other live networking functions. These sites allow physicians to discuss common frustrations from the professional to the personal.

While there is an abundance of options for physicians seeking an online community, one network has emerged as the clear leader—Sermo.com. with more than 112,000 physician members.

While the network itself is exclusively for physicians, Sermo makes a profit by selling data to healthcare companies who are interested in learning what physicians think.

Like Sermo, MedScape claims over 100,000 members, but due to their open registration process, it is impossible to know how many of those members are physicians. On a smaller scale, sites with a distinct niche seem to be faring well with the audiences they target. MomMD has over 8,000 registered members and has established a solid reputation among female physicians. Online networks targeting specialists, such as CardiologyRounds.com, are also gaining some traction.

On the other hand, it seems many social networks for physicians could be here today and gone tomorrow.

An increasing number of physicians are flocking to exclusive online communities. The advice and information resulting from the discourse within these communities appears to be benefiting everyone involved—from the physicians themselves, to the patients they treat, to the companies "listening" to the conversations, to the public at large. For this reason, it seems these communities will continue to grow.

Online focus groups

Different market research managers mean different things when they talk about online focus groups (Digital MR, 2012).[12] There are two main forms of focus group: synchronous or asynchronous.

- *Synchronous*: All participants are online at the same time.
- *Asynchronous*: The focus group members participate in the conversation when they are online.

Synchronous focus groups can be divided in four main forms:

1. Virtual Focus Group
    This form involves six to eight participants who are online at the same time using video and audio to communicate with each other and with the moderator. Duration 60–90 minutes.
2. Chat Group
    The six to eight participants communicate with each other and with the moderator by typing in a chat box. No video or audio is used. Duration 60–90 minutes.
3. Enhanced Chat Group
    This is the same as the Chat Group for the participants the only difference is that the moderator alone uses video and audio.

4. Mini Group
     This can take the form of any of the first three types described above with the only difference that there are fewer participants, that is, four to five.

Asynchronous focus groups can be divided in two main forms:

1. Bulletin Board. This form involves 10–20 participants who participate when they are online by typing their responses to moderator questions that are posted in advance. This discussion may last from four to five days to a few weeks. Some call this a short-term community.
2. Enhanced Bulletin Board. The same as a Bulletin Board but with the additional possibility for all to post photos or video clips in addition to their typed comments.

Other online qualitative research forms that do not fall under the description of focus groups in our view are:

- online in-depth interviews using chat or video and audio;
- online diaries;
- video or photo diaries;
- online diads and triads.

The main difference that focus group discussions (FGDs) have over the above methods is that more than four people are leading a discussion about a subject whereas the above are mainly one-to-one discussions.

In 2009, Sermo has launched Sermo Panels, a service aimed at ad agencies, PR shops and market research firms as well as its pharma industry clients.

"We're faster than anyone out there now, and they're getting deep feedback from our physicians," said Greg Shenk, marketing director at Sermo. "You don't have to worry about travel or logistics, and it's an asynchronous discussion, so you don't have to have doctors here from 2 p.m. to 5 p.m."

Participating physicians commit to putting a set amount of time into the discussion—usually 90 minutes over three to five days, said Shenk—and get an honoraria, typically $150 to $300 per panel. Sermo doesn't take a cut of that, instead charging a lump sum, typically around $16,000 per full panel, or $10,000 for the no-frills "express" version. That offering, aimed at smaller clients and cash-strapped agencies, leaves the analysis to the client.

Market researchers can query the focus groups in real-time about brand messaging and new strategies, and can also use the panels for qualifying product uptake after a launch, and tracking physician behavior and perception of a brand or a new digital tool over time, among other things.

Table 4.2 Appropriate form of focus group projects

IN DEPTH INTERVIEWS (IDIs) OR DIARIES
If the subject is sensitive or if we do not want the participants to be influenced by what other people say or show

VIRTUAL FOCUS GROUPS OR CHAT GROUPS
If the subject requires a more dynamic discussion with more interaction among the participants

SIMPLE CHAT GROUPS OR BULLETIN BOARDS
If participants are not very technologically savvy

ASYNCHRONOUS METHODS
For very low incidence and difficult to find participants

Choosing the right form of focus group discussion

Choosing the most appropriate FGD is at the basis of the value and insightfulness of the findings you will get. It depends on the kind of topic (that is, sensitive), the level of needed interaction, and the importance of influence among participants. Table 3.1 lists some general guidelines on how to choose the appropriate form or method for your project.

Recruitment

Recruitment for online focus groups is a little different than for face-to-face ones. The traditional way is to go to a qualitative recruitment agency, provide the profile, agree on the incentive and then wait for the group participants to arrive on the set date. Recruitment can be done through consumer panels but this affects the quality of respondents: panelists may participate in surveys purely for the incentives and do whatever it takes to qualify for a research project. Another consideration is that some participants have great difficulties with the technology, even after coaching on the phone they are still challenged. This is why the software has to be very intuitive and very simple.

Moderator

If you are an end-user of market research you probably already know the importance of the moderator. This is the person who will write the discussion guide based on your objectives, facilitate the discussion and write the report. A moderator will ideally be an experienced qualitative researcher. Academic disciplines that offer themselves for this job are Psychology and Sociology but they are not a pre-condition for a good moderator. There are certain moderating techniques (such as Projective Techniques) that are suitable for certain objectives and the moderator has to know when to use these methods.

Insights

Sometimes focus groups are used as a pre-cursor to a quantitative survey in order to provide support in the questionnaire design and sometimes they are the only research that will need to meet certain marketing objectives. The data can be available to the researcher as audio or video files, as a transcript of the discussion and uploaded images or video clips. In order for the researcher to be in a position to deliver valuable customer insights, they need to have a thorough understanding of the research objectives. These objectives need to be designed to be action-oriented so that the insights in the research report will lead to actions that will in turn lead to a business benefit.

> **"Listening and turning mountains of information into fresh insights is key to deliver greater value to customers."**

Notes

1 Letizia Affinito and John Mark (2015), *Socialize Your Patient Engagement Strategy: How Social Media and Mobile Apps Can Boost Health Outcomes*. Abingdon: Routledge.
2 P. Kotler and G. Armstrong (2014), *Principles of Marketing*, 15th edition. Harlow: Pearson Education, pp. 122–148.
3 Digital MR (2017), "Choosing the right social media monitoring tool for market research." Integral reproduction with permission. [online]. Available at https://www.digital-mr.com/blog/view/choosing-right-social-media-monitoring-tool-market-research [Accessed March 12, 2018].
4 Michalis Michael and Divya Radhakrishnan (2017), "How to integrate data from online surveys with social listening & analytics."
5 N.K. Baym (2007), "The new shape of online community: The example of Swedish independent music fandom." *First Monday*, 12(8) [online]. Available at http://firstmonday.org/ojs/index.php/fm/article/view/1978/1853 [Accessed December 22, 2014].
6 V. Di Mauro (2012), "Online community decision: Public, private or hybrid?" [online]. Available at www.leadernetworks.com/2012/01/online-community-decision-public.html [Accessed December 22, 2014].
7 Digital MR (2012), "How to benefit from private online communities (POCs)." Integral reproduction.
8 Elsevier Health Sciences (2012), "Social media—general practitioners and medical specialists—Spain, UK, Germany, Brazil, Italy and France."
9 K. Hancock (2012), "Redefining the message: Online Qual guides health care foundation to shift its focus." *Quirk's Marketing Research Review*, 30–32.
10 Digital MR (2012), "How to benefit from private online communities (POCs)." Integral reproduction with permission.
11 MD Search.com (2009), "Physicians and online communities." [online]. Available at https://www.mdsearch.com/physician-social-networks [Accessed March 12, 2018].
12 Digital MR (2012), "How to make online focus groups work for you." Integral reproduction with permission.

Developing a data strategy to gain physician insights for better decision-making

5

In this chapter, we will explore how managers gain insights into physicians/ patients' needs and the health system. We look at how organizations develop and manage data about important health system elements: physicians, patients, competitors, products and digital programs. To succeed in today's health system organizations must know how to turn mountains of information into fresh insights that will help them deliver greater value to customers.

We'll begin our journey with a **leading case history** on patient empowerment in action at Intermountain Healthcare, a not-for-profit health system based in Salt Lake City, Utah, with 22 hospitals, a broad range of clinics and services, about 1,400 employed primary care and secondary care physicians at more than 185 clinics in the Intermountain Medical Group, and health insurance plans from SelectHealth.

In the mid-1990s, everyone knew that healthcare organizations across the United States were plagued by wasteful spending.[1] The question for Intermountain Healthcare was where to start looking for savings internally. Data analyses quickly identified the most promising targets: 104 of the 1,440 clinical conditions that Intermountain treated accounted for 95% of the care it provided, and two services—newborn delivery and treatment of ischemic heart disease—accounted for 21% of its work.

Quality-improvement teams focused first on those two services. Armed with a sophisticated electronic health record (EHR) and a separate information technology system that detailed the costs of activities, the teams used evidence-based guidelines and the experience of Intermountain's physicians to redesign clinical workflows. The top executives, the board of trustees, physicians and nurses all worked together to support the drive to improve care. Today more than 60 services have been revamped, and Intermountain is recognized as a national leader in quality improvement and cost management. None of it would have been possible without its IT systems.

This example is impressive. Unfortunately, it is still a rarity. The more common story in healthcare is one of large IT investments but little to show for them. Many healthcare organizations are suffering more pain than gain as they struggle to integrate new IT systems into their operations. For example, in January 2017, MD Anderson Cancer Center announced that it would lay off 900 employees, or about 5% of its workforce, largely because of financial losses attributable to a new EHR system. More broadly, efforts to persuade healthcare organizations to share information continue to lag, as do efforts to enable different IT systems to communicate with one another, causing data to remain "stuck" within siloed databases.

Before focusing on data it is important to highlight that one of the biggest and most frequent mistakes is that historically the adoption and management of healthcare IT has been left to an organization's chief information officer and other technical personnel.

Indeed, two key constituencies outside of technical personnel—senior leaders and clinicians—must play significant roles. Leaders are crucial because they will have to enlist clinicians in the cause by persuading them that the effective use of IT is central to delivering higher quality. The urgent need to reduce healthcare costs has led many leaders to become preoccupied with that objective. The happy reality is that improving clinical work processes can achieve both lower costs and higher quality, and we'll discuss later what it takes to use IT systems to do this.

Most importantly, the pledge to improve quality should be more than words; it must be translated into visible practices.

How managers gain insights into physicians/patients' needs and the health system

Based on a recent survey conducted by Health Catalyst[2] which interviewed members of the College of Healthcare Information Management Executives (CHIME), 54% of respondents rated healthcare analytics as their highest IT priority, followed by investments in population health initiatives (42%). More than 90% of the survey respondents view analytics as "extremely important" or "very important" to their organization within the next 1–3 years, when a combination of government requirements and market pressures will force many of these issues to the forefront.

Analytics is important for tackling a variety of healthcare trends. The respondents also rated the importance of healthcare trends that are accelerating the adoption of analytics. Survey takers ranked population health management highest at 84%, followed by quality improvement (79%) and accountable care (68%). Other important initiatives ranked by survey takers included the need for cost reduction (63%), for a "single version of the truth" (59%), for better reporting (54%) and for research (17%).

In order to prioritize quality improvement over cost cutting it will be critical to make data collection easier and better. As a matter of fact, having high-quality data at the right time is critical to tracking and measuring outcome improvement. Yet the data collection methods that most healthcare organizations use are inefficient, administratively burdensome, and likely to produce errors.

It is nearly impossible to speak to a group of clinicians without the conversation quickly turning to the time-consuming task of gathering medical information and entering it into a new IT system. A time and motion study published in the Annals of Internal Medicine in 2016 found that physicians spend one to two hours each night after their workday mostly on EHR tasks. This addition to their already heavy workload is contributing to the epidemic of physician burnout in the United States and worldwide. And studies show that these problems cause physicians to take shortcuts such as copying and pasting notes and rapidly clicking through alerts, undermining the quality of the data that's collected.

In response, many organizations now employ medical scribes to enter information into EHR systems on behalf of clinicians. Yet the awkwardness of having a third party in an examination room—not to mention the added cost—makes the use of medical scribes controversial. Moreover, patient information that is gathered and entered into the system in this manner is prone to error.

The remedy: Shift data collection from an "event" that takes time and may be performed inaccurately to one that occurs "in the background" as clinicians and patients engage in their natural activities. The retail industry shows what's possible. During the past few decades, retail has experienced two significant shifts with respect to who collects data and how. One example is checkout. Cashiers used to have to key the price of each item into a cash register. The introduction of bar code scanners sharply reduced the amount of time cashiers spent on that task, decreased data-entry mistakes, and greatly improved inventory management. Next, it became possible for many customers to scan their own items. Amazon is now taking things one step further by piloting its Amazon Go brick-and-mortar store, which eliminates checkout lines altogether. Instead, a passive data-collection system relies on computer vision, deep-learning algorithms, and sensors to automatically read what exiting customers have in their shopping baskets. Other retailers, including Kroger and Apple, are experimenting with analogous models.

In healthcare, a similar transition has begun but is moving slowly. One trend is to shift the job of collecting information from clinicians to patients. For example, after a primary care physician and a patient agree to address a clinical goal such as reducing blood pressure or blood sugar levels, they can enter that goal and the associated treatment plan into one of the health-monitoring apps offered by a number of companies. Patients then measure and report their activity and clinical information on a regular basis through the app. In some cases, data collected by the patient at home is automatically shared with his or her clinician. One example is the Hypertension Digital Medicine (HDM) program developed by Ochsner Health System. Through smartphone technology, blood pressure readings taken remotely by patients are fed directly into Ochsner's EHR system, allowing physicians to review data between visits and course-correct a patient's care plan. In a controlled trial reported in the American Journal of Medicine, 71% of participants brought their blood pressure down to the normal range within 90 days, compared to only 31% in the control group. The patients using HDM also reported 10% higher satisfaction with their healthcare.

Ultimately, the goal should be to move to truly passive data collection. Some pioneers are using passive collection to track operational issues related to workflow and resource utilization. Mayo Clinic developed a real-time location system (RTLS) that uses radio frequency identification tags and sensors to track staff, patients, and equipment in its emergency department. This data allowed the department to better understand how care was delivered, identify operational barriers, and fix workflow issues. Then the information was used to develop systems for automatically collecting process-quality metrics (such as the time between a patient's registering at the emergency department's front desk and being put in a bed and seen by a clinician) and automatically reporting that information to government agencies and regulatory bodies. (See "How RFID Technology Improves Hospital Care.")

When redesigning the new and expanded emergency room at the Mayo Clinic's Saint Mary's Hospital in Rochester, Minnesota, Mayo leaders didn't just want to add more rooms and square feet. They saw it as an opportunity to completely transform the operation to improve care and the patient experience and to lower costs. To that end, they decided to have a team study how care is delivered, identify the barriers to smooth operations and fix the barriers. In other words, they created a living lab of the clinic's largest emergency department.

The successful experience illustrates the role that relatively simple technology (e.g., an RFID system) and a multidiscipline team of clinicians and people from other fields can play in improving the quality and cost of care delivery processes and the steps that can ease the way to applying such an approach. The project was launched in 2013, and the RFID system was rolled out in stages starting in the summer of 2015. It was fully integrated into emergency room operations at St. Mary's during the fourth quarter of 2015.

The system is reducing the time that staff members spend finding equipment and each other, and it informs them when a colleague is attending a patient and shouldn't be interrupted. Similarly, family members are now directed more quickly to patients. And misplaced equipment can now be easily located and returned to its correct place. All this is allowing the clinical staff to spend more of their time on activities that benefit patients. Mayo is now evaluating the use of RFID systems in other areas of patient care.

Here is some advice for carrying out such a program:

- *Create a multidiscipline team.* The team that implemented the initiative was led by a physician and a scientist-engineer, and its members were drawn from Mayo's Emergency Department (ED) and the Clinic's Robert D. and Patricia E. Kern Center for the Science of Health Care Delivery. This Emergency Department-Clinical Engineering Learning Laboratory (ED-CELL) team comprises physicians, nurses, other health professionals, systems engineers, scientists, informaticians, IT personnel and project managers.
- *Use technology to identify and address barriers.* The new infrastructure was a real-time-location (RTL) system with state-of-the-art location sensors and devices that use radio frequency identification (RFID) technology to track the movement of and locate patients, staff and equipment. High-density RFID readers were installed in the ceilings. All patients receive RFID wristbands when they register. Staff members have RFID chips in their badges. And equipment is tagged with discrete RFID stickers. All of the RFID tags are "passive technology," meaning that the individual tags don't need power. The ED-CELL team developed software to provide the stream of RFID data to frontline staff in a usable manner.
- *Address potential obstacles early.* One obvious issue was whether the RFID technology would interfere with the ECG machine, monitoring equipment and the overhead communication and paging systems. The team conducted systematic testing and ensured that it did not adversely affect the functioning of other ED equipment and devices. Another issue was

potential staff and patient concerns about wearables and privacy. The ED-CELL team sought out the insights and perspectives of all stakeholders before the launch of the RTL system. It held a series of town hall meetings with the St. Mary's ED clinical staff to explain the scope and benefits of the project, answer questions, and obtain feedback. Frontline caregivers often react to new data-collecting technologies with caution and resistance. So the team was not surprised when members of the ED staff were concerned that their every move would be monitored. Some were worried that the data collected would be used for their performance reviews. In particular, the staff members were anxious that they might be tracked during breaks and time off the unit. In subsequent meetings and one-on-one discussions, the team reassured the staff that the system was intended to be a "clinical tool" and would not track them in the restrooms or during breaks. When staff members are outside the clinical area, they are displayed as "out of department." Patients were less concerned. When the ED-CELL team asked members of patient and family advisory councils of Emergency Medicine and the Kern Center how they would feel about having an RFID chip in their wristbands, their immediate response was: "Don't you do it already?" From them, the team learned that patients often worry about being lost in the maze of hallways, being forgotten after registering, and missing their announcement in ED waiting rooms. So they embraced the idea of location devices. The team also sought the input of various departments, including human resources, legal and compliance, and ethics consultants, and the approvals of key internal committees including clinical practice, location services and information technology.

- *Integrate the system into the workflow.* From a technical standpoint, several steps need to be taken to seamlessly integrate RFID into the existing workflow. For instance, when a patient is registered at the ED's front desk, a wristband with a unique ID is wrapped on his or her wrist and the RTL system is notified that this unique ID belongs to such patient through a "commissioning process." The RTL system was integrated with existing information technology systems to provide a visual display of the locations of patients, key staff members (e.g., the physician and supervisory "charge" nurse), and equipment, and how long each has been at the current location. The location and duration information for all patients, staff members and equipment can also be obtained using an RTL system search tool.

An important lesson of this initiative is that you cannot rely on technology alone to bring about innovation and change in a fast-paced environment. Creating an environment that nurtures collaboration across disciplines, ongoing engagement and continuous learning is just as crucial. Employing a scientific approach to improvement and having a team of scientists, clinicians and engineers work with the local clinical staff at the patient's bedside is a powerful way to bring about change.[3]

Similarly, Rush University Medical Center in Chicago built a new outpatient practice with RTLS sensors for each room, clinician, patient and piece of equipment. The system alerts staff when a patient leaves his or her exam room, eliminating the need for a practice manager to inform cleaning staff that a room needs to be serviced and preventing awkward interruptions of patients who are still dressing after an appointment. The time saved per patient is relatively small—perhaps just one minute. But over the course of a day, the total savings allow clinicians to see more patients, thereby improving productivity.

Over time, as passive data collection technologies become less costly and as clinicians and patients become more comfortable with them, the benefits will increase. This will help organizations justify the upfront cost and make it easier to overcome hurdles such as employee concerns about being monitored.

How to turn mountains of information into fresh customer insights that will help them deliver greater value to customers

Once we have made data collection easier and better, the next important step is to turning data into actionable information.

Persuading clinicians to engage with a new IT system—and making it less burdensome for them to do so—is only half the battle. Turning the data collected into actionable information is also vital and requires senior leadership's support. One of the most critical tasks for a leader is to set expectations for how the system will be structured. The focus here is not about the technical specifications but about organizational or cultural guidelines for using the data to support daily care-related activities.

A key step is establishing a core data warehouse for the organization and getting clinicians to understand its importance. When presenting the case to the staff of New York University Langone Health, one of the nation's premier academic medical centers devoted to patient care, education and research, Dr. Grossman, the center CEO in 2017, emphasized the value of having a *single source of truth* across inpatient facilities, outpatient centers, and the medical school. In the process of developing the data warehouse, various parties at NYU Langone Health that were previously protective of their "backyard" and information were forced to work together. Disputes over which of several data sources were accurate ended, and Grossman persuaded department chairs to start using tools such as data dashboards to assess what was (and was not) working across departments. Over time, as the benefits of the resulting transparency became apparent, clinical leaders' initial skepticism about the IT system subsided. Departments would receive data on quality metrics for peer departments within NYU Langone Health (the rates of hospital-acquired infection in different parts of the hospital, patients' length of stay, and so on), and they could then determine whether and how to change their own workflows.

Beyond encouraging the development of the necessary data infrastructure, senior leaders must also help *establish a vision* for how the collected data will be used to improve productivity. In many cases, pursuing the vision may involve supporting the creation of entirely new measures of performance.

Finally, it is critical to forge new operating and business models. In its 2012 report *Best Care at Lower Cost: The Path to Continuously Learning Health Care in America*, the Institute of Medicine (IOM) highlighted ways to leverage IT to improve the US healthcare system. Five years later, the first recommendation— the creation of digital infrastructure to capture clinical, care process, and financial data—is approaching completion.

The IOM's second recommendation was to make data available to clinicians when they are deciding how to treat patients. This is being done sporadically. For example, Intermountain recently partnered with Cerner to create a flexible clinical-support system containing protocols that can be easily updated with the latest knowledge. To facilitate the right inputs, Intermountain's clinical-development teams continuously monitor the various specialties' evidence-based practice guidelines and are translating them into IT tools that assist medical personnel as they work.

Besides acquiring the necessary hardware and software, leaders must make complementary changes in their operating and business models to generate and capture value. Of primary importance is investment in dedicated information technology and analytics staff—individuals tasked with managing the IT system or analyzing the data it contains.

Specialized teams of clinical personnel are also needed to translate the insights from the analyses into better ways of providing care.

The data that robust IT systems can provide also plays a crucial role in securing clinicians' support for workflow changes. For example, when Grossman first shared a dashboard with NYU Langone's clinical leaders, he heard complaints about the quality and consistency of data. Instead of letting that derail the project, he put the onus on the leaders, telling them to either work with IT to fix the data or accept the results. At the end of this process, the data was considered the single source of truth throughout the medical center and the basis for future analytical efforts. This made it easier for the organization to track metrics consistently. The dashboard now helps clinical leaders work with frontline staff to implement interventions to improve care delivery, track what is and isn't working, persuade resistant clinicians to adopt new protocols, and reduce variation in treatment practices.

Beyond these workforce and operational changes, healthcare organizations will have to rethink their business models in order to capture the full value of their IT investments.

How organizations develop and manage data about important health system elements: physicians, patients, competitors, products, and digital programs

The healthcare industry historically has generated large amounts of data which is mostly stored in hard copy form. Indeed, the current trend is toward rapid digitization of these large amounts of data.[4]

Driven by mandatory requirements and the potential to improve the quality of healthcare delivery meanwhile reducing the costs, these massive quantities of data (known as 'big data') hold the promise of supporting a wide range of medical and healthcare functions, including, among others, patient empowerment, clinical decision support, disease surveillance, and population health management.[5,6,7,8]

By definition, big data in healthcare refers to electronic health data sets so large and complex that they are difficult (or impossible) to manage with traditional software and/or hardware; nor can they be easily managed with traditional or common data-management tools and methods.[9] Big data in healthcare is overwhelming not only because of its volume but also because of the diversity of data types and the speed at which it must be managed.[10] It includes clinical data from:

- Computerized provider order entry (CPOE)
- Clinical decision support systems (physician's written notes and prescriptions, medical imaging, laboratory, pharmacy, insurance, and other administrative data)
- Patient data in electronic patient records (EPRs)
- Machine generated/sensor data (i.e. from monitoring vital signs; social media posts, etc.)

By discovering associations and understanding patterns and trends within the data, big data analytics has the potential to improve care, save lives and lower costs.

When big data is synthesized and analyzed—and associations, patterns and trends revealed—healthcare providers and other stakeholders in the healthcare delivery system can develop more thorough and insightful diagnoses, treatments and patient empowerment, resulting, one would expect, in higher quality care at lower costs and in better outcomes overall.[11]

Big data analytics in healthcare

What exactly is big data? A report delivered to the U.S. Congress in August 2012 defines big data as "large volumes of high velocity, complex, and variable data that require advanced techniques and technologies to enable the capture, storage, distribution, management and analysis of the information."[12] Big data encompasses such characteristics as variety, velocity and, with respect specifically to healthcare, veracity.[13,14,15] Existing analytical techniques can be applied to the vast amount of existing (but currently unanalyzed) patient-related health and medical data to reach a deeper understanding of outcomes, which then can be applied at the point of care. Ideally, individual and population data would inform each physician and his/her patient during the decision-making process and help determine the most appropriate treatment option for that particular patient.

Like big data in healthcare, the analytics associated with big data is described by four primary characteristics:

Volume: The volume of data that companies manage skyrocketed around 2012, when they began collecting more than 3 million pieces of data every data. Since then, this volume doubles about every 40 months.

Velocity: In addition to managing data, companies need that information to flow quickly—as close to real-time as possible. The data have to be available at the right time to make appropriate business decisions.

Variety: A company can obtain data from many different sources: from in-house devices to smartphone GPS technology or what people are saying on social networks. The importance of these sources of information varies depending on the nature of the business.

Veracity (quality): We have all the data, but could we be missing something? Are the data "clean" and accurate? Do they really have something to offer?

Value: Value sits at the top of the big data pyramid and refers to the ability to transform a tsunami of data into valuable management decisions.

As the nature of health data has evolved, so too have analytics techniques scaled up to the complex and sophisticated analytics necessary to accommodate volume, velocity, variety and value. Gone are the days of data collected exclusively in electronic health records and other structured formats. Increasingly, the data is in multimedia format and unstructured. The enormous variety of data—structured, unstructured and semi-structured—is a dimension that makes healthcare data both interesting and challenging.

Structured data is data that can be easily stored, queried, recalled, analyzed and manipulated by machine. Historically, in healthcare, structured and semi-structured data includes instrument readings and data generated by the ongoing conversion of paper records to electronic health and medical records. Historically, the point of care generated *unstructured data*: office medical records, handwritten nurse and doctor notes, hospital admission and discharge records, paper prescriptions, radiograph films, MRI, CT and other images.

Already, new data streams—structured and unstructured—are cascading into the healthcare realm from fitness devices, genetics and genomics, social media research and other sources. But relatively little of this data can presently be captured, stored and organized so that it can be manipulated by computers and analyzed for useful information. Healthcare applications in particular need more efficient ways to combine and convert varieties of data including automating conversion from structured to unstructured data.

The structured data in EMRs and EHRs include familiar input record fields such as patient name, data of birth, address, physician's name, hospital name and address, treatment reimbursement codes, and other information easily coded into and handled by automated databases. The need to field-code data at the point of care for electronic handling is a major barrier to acceptance of EMRs by physicians and nurses, who lose the natural language ease of entry and understanding that handwritten notes provide. On the other hand, most providers agree that an easy way to reduce prescription errors is to use digital entries rather than handwritten scripts.

The potential of big data in healthcare lies in combining traditional data with new forms of data, both individually and on a population level. We are already seeing data sets from a multitude of sources support faster and more reliable research and discovery. If, for example, pharmaceutical developers could integrate population clinical data sets with genomics data, this development could facilitate those developers gaining approvals on more and better drug therapies more quickly than in the past and, more importantly, expedite distribution to the right patients.[16] The prospects for all areas of healthcare are infinite.

The '5Vs' are an appropriate starting point for a discussion about big data analytics in healthcare. But there are other issues to consider, such as the number of architectures and platforms, and the dominance of the open source paradigm in the availability of tools. Consider, too, the challenge of developing methodologies and the need for user-friendly interfaces.

While the overall cost of hardware and software is declining, these issues have to be addressed to harness and maximize the potential of big data analytics in healthcare.

At minimum, a big data analytics platform in healthcare must support the key functions necessary for processing the data. The criteria for platform evaluation may include availability, continuity, ease of use, scalability, ability to manipulate at different levels of granularity, privacy and security enablement, and quality assurance.[17,18,19] In addition, while most platforms currently available are open source, the typical advantages and limitations of open source platforms apply. To succeed, big data analytics in healthcare needs to be packaged so it is menu-driven, user-friendly and transparent. Real-time big data analytics is a key requirement in healthcare. The lag between data collection and processing has to be addressed.

The dynamic availability of numerous analytics algorithms, models and methods in a pull-down type of menu is also necessary for large-scale adoption. The important managerial issues of ownership, governance and standards have to be considered. And woven through these issues are those of continuous data acquisition and data cleansing.

Healthcare data is rarely standardized, often fragmented, or generated in legacy IT systems with incompatible formats.[20] This great challenge needs to be addressed as well.

In conclusion, big data analytics has the potential to transform the way healthcare providers use sophisticated technologies to gain insight from their clinical and other data repositories and make informed decisions. In the future we'll see the rapid, widespread implementation and use of big data analytics across the healthcare organization and the healthcare industry. To that end, the several challenges highlighted above, must be addressed. As big data analytics becomes more mainstream, issues such as guaranteeing privacy, safeguarding security, establishing standards and governance, and continually improving the tools and technologies will garner attention. Big data analytics and applications in healthcare are at a nascent stage of development, but rapid advances in platforms and tools can accelerate their maturing process.

Transformation of the healthcare data analyst's role

As analytics is increasingly recognized as a critical enabler of healthcare transformation, the role of data analyst has taken center stage. Health Catalyst conducted a recent survey of attendees at the Healthcare Analytics Summit (HAS) session: "Getting the most out of your data analyst." The survey data showed how important data analysts are to their organizations. Ninety percent of respondents claimed that the role of data analyst is either very important or important.[21]

At the same time, the survey revealed just how little time these analysts are able to spend fulfilling their job title: analyzing data. In fact, 79% of data analysts spend more than half of their time gathering versus analyzing data.

For data-driven healthcare transformation to succeed, this paradigm must shift. To deliver their true value, analysts need to spend the majority of their time analyzing data. The flow of data is becoming the lifeblood of organizations— and deriving meaningful insights from this data will be the key to survival in a changing industry.

Specifically, when dealing with new digital tools development and adoption, if practitioners from data science and design work together and learn each other's art they will produce better outcomes.

Let's take as an example Rise Science, a young start-up using a combination of sleep data and user inputs, to satisfy everyone's individual sleep needs, which came to IDEO with a challenge: making it easier for college and professional athletes (their target customers), to find insights related to their sleep and change their behavior so that they played at peak performance.[22] Rise Science was sure they just needed easier-to-read charts and graphs.

As IDEO designers and Rise's data scientists spent time with players and coaches, they found out that Rise didn't have a data visualization problem, they had a user-experience problem. Charts and graphs were far less important than knowing when to go to bed each night and when to wake up the next morning. Within a few weeks, the charts and graphs moved into the background of their app and an alarm clock and a chat tool took center stage.

In the 18 months since relaunching their service, Rise Science has signed up over 15 of the most elite pro and collegiate sports teams, as well as several companies who hope to improve employee performance and well-being through better sleep habits.

This example shows how human-centered data science can result from interdisciplinary teams incorporating design thinking into their approach. Instead of a version of data science that is narrowly focused on researching new statistical models or building better data visualizations, a design-thinking approach recognizes data scientists as creative problem solvers.

A new framework for building a robust data strategy

Having a Chief Data Officer and a data-management function is a start, but neither can be fully effective in the absence of a coherent strategy for organizing, governing, analyzing and deploying an organization's information assets. Drawing on their implementation experience at the global insurer AIG (where DalleMule is the CDO) and their study of half a dozen other large companies where its elements have been applied, Leandro DalleMule and Thomas H. Davenport[23] have developed a new framework for building a robust data strategy that can be applied across industries and levels of data maturity.

Their framework addresses two key issues: It helps companies clarify the primary purpose of their data, and it guides them in strategic data-management.

Unlike other approaches this one requires companies to make considered trade-offs between "defensive" and "offensive" uses of data and between control and flexibility in its use. This framework not only promotes the efficient use of data and allocation of resources but also helps companies design their data-management activities to support their overall strategy.

Data defense and offense are differentiated by distinct business objectives and the activities designed to address them.

Data defense, typically used in healthcare, is about minimizing downside risk. Activities include ensuring compliance with regulations (such as rules governing data privacy and the integrity of financial reports), using analytics to detect and limit fraud, and building systems to prevent theft. Defensive efforts also ensure the integrity of data flowing through a company's internal systems by identifying, standardizing, and governing authoritative data sources, such as fundamental customer and supplier information or sales data, in a "single source of truth."

Data offense (typically used in consumer goods) focuses on supporting business objectives such as increasing revenue, profitability and customer satisfaction. It typically includes activities that generate customer insights (data analysis and modeling, for example) or integrate disparate customer and market data to support managerial decision-making through, for instance, interactive dashboards.

Offensive activities tend to be most relevant for customer-focused business functions such as sales and marketing and are often more real-time than is defensive work, with its concentration on legal, financial, compliance and IT concerns. (An exception would be data fraud protection, in which seconds count and real-time analytics smarts are critical.)

Every company needs both offense and defense to succeed, but getting the balance right is tricky. Putting equal emphasis on the two is optimal for some companies. But for many others it's wiser to favor one or the other.

Some company or environmental factors may influence the direction of data strategy: Strong regulation in an industry (financial services or healthcare, for example) would move the organization toward defense; strong competition for customers would shift it toward offense. The challenge for CDOs and the rest of the C-suite is to establish the appropriate trade-offs between defense and offense and to ensure the best balance in support of the company's overall strategy.

Decisions about these trade-offs are rooted in the fundamental dichotomy between standardizing data and keeping it more flexible. The more uniform data is, the easier it becomes to execute defensive processes, such as complying with regulatory requirements and implementing data-access controls. The more flexible data is—that is, the more readily it can be transformed or interpreted to meet specific business needs—the more useful it is in offense. Balancing offense and defense, then, requires balancing data control and flexibility.

The key innovation of Leandro DalleMule and Thomas H. Davenport's framework is this: It requires flexible data and information architectures that permit both single source of truth (a logical, often virtual and cloud-based repository that contains one authoritative copy of all crucial data, such as customer, supplier, and product details) and multiple versions of the truth (resulting from the business-specific transformation of data into information) to support a defensive-offensive approach to data strategy.

Although the SSOT-MVOTs model is conceptually straightforward, it requires robust data controls, standards, governance and technology. Ideally, senior executives will actively participate on data governance boards and committees. Typically, enterprise CDOs and CTOs lead data and technology governance processes, and business and technology managers in functions and units are the primary participants. What's critical is that single sources of the truth remain unique and valid, and that multiple versions of the truth diverge from the original source only in carefully controlled ways.

So, how to strike the best balance between defense and offense and between control and flexibility? Whereas the CEO—often with the CIO—is ultimately responsible for a company's data strategy, the CDO commonly conceives it and leads its development and execution. The CDO must determine the right trade-offs while dynamically adjusting the balance by leveraging the SSOT and MVOTs architectures.

It's rare to find an organization—especially a large, complex one—in which data is both tightly controlled and flexibly used. With few exceptions, CDOs find that their best data strategy emphasizes either defense and control (which depends on a robust SSOT) or offense and flexibility (enabled by MVOTs). Devoting equal attention to offense and defense is sometimes optimal, but in general it's unwise to default to a 50/50 split rather than making considered, strategic trade-offs. To determine a company's current and desired positions on the offense-defense spectrum, the CDO must bear in mind, among other things, the company's overall strategy, its regulatory environment, the data capabilities of its competitors, the maturity of its data-management practices, and the size of its data budget. For example, insurance and financial services and healthcare organizations typically operate in heavily regulated environments, which argues for an emphasis on data defense. Retailers, operating in a less-regulated environment where intense competition requires robust customer analytics, might emphasize offense.

In their article which I strongly invite you to ready entirely, Leandro DalleMule and Thomas H. Davenport present the tool "Assess Your Strategy Position" which offers diagnostic questions that can help CDOs place their companies on the offense-defense spectrum and gauge whether their data strategy aligns with their corporate strategy. Determining an organization's current and desired positions on the spectrum will force executives to make trade-offs between offensive and defensive investments. Of course, this tool is not a precise measure. CDOs should use the results to inform data strategy and discussions with other C-level executives.

Assess Your Strategy Position

To determine where your firm falls on the data-strategy spectrum, select the eight objectives that are most important to your business. (Select only eight.)

Please check all that apply in this category.

- Optimize existing strong bench of analysts and data scientists
- Create new products and services
- Improve revenue through cross-sell, pricing, and expanded customer base
- Leverage new sources of data, internal or external
- Rationalize multiple sources of the same data and information
- Generate return on investments in big data and analytics infrastructure
- Improve IT infrastructure and reduce data-related costs (number of databases, etc.)
- Reduce general operating expenses and streamline business processes
- Monetize the value of the company's data; use internal data as a product or service
- Develop analytics and digital capabilities
- Improve the quality of data
- Use sophisticated, real-time or near real-time analytics for business
- Mitigate operational risks such as data breaks, fraud, etc.
- Respond rapidly to competitors and market changes
- Meet industry regulatory requirements
- Prevent cyber attacks and data breaches

"Data collection must shift from an *event* that takes time and may be performed inaccurately to one that occurs *in the background* as clinicians and patients engage in their natural activities."

Notes

1 Nikhil R. Sahni, Robert S. Huckman, Anuraag Chigurupati and David M. Cutler (2017), "The IT transformation health care needs." *Harvard Business Review.* [online]. Available at https://hbr.org/2017/11/the-it-transformation-health-care-needs [Accessed January 23, 2018].

2 Dr. John Haughom et al. (2017), "The changing role of healthcare data analysts—How our most successful clients are embracing healthcare transformation (executive report)." [online]. Available at https://www.healthcatalyst.com/the-changing-role-of-healthcare-data-analysts/ [Accessed March 14, 2018].

3 Kalyan S. Pasupathy and Thomas R. Hellmich (2015), "How RFID technology improves hospital care." *Harvard Business Review.* [online]. Available at https://hbr.org/2015/12/how-rfid-technology-improves-hospital-care [Accessed January 23, 2018].

4 Wullianallur Raghupathi and Viju Raghupathi (2014), "Big data analytics in healthcare: Promise and potential." *Health Information Science and Systems*, 2(3). [online]. Available at https://www.ncbi.nlm.nih.gov/pmc/articles/PMC4341817/ [Accessed January 23, 2018].

5 C. Burghard (2012), "Big data and analytics key to accountable care success." *IDC Health Insights* #HI237529. [online]. Available at https://www.coursehero.com/file/14345607/Big-Data-and-Analytics-Key-to/ [Accessed January 23, 2018].

6 A. Dembosky (2012), "Data prescription for better healthcare." *Financial Times*, p. 19.

7 B. Feldman, E.M. Martin and T. Skotnes (2012), "Big data in healthcare hype and hope." *Dr. Bonnie 360.* [online]. Available at https://www.ghdonline.org/uploads/big-data-in-healthcare_B_Kaplan_2012.pdf [Accessed January 23, 2018].

8 Lorraine M. Fernandes, Michele O'Connor and Victoria Weaver (2012), "Big data, bigger outcomes." *Journal of AHIMA*, 83(10), 38–43.

9 Frost and Sullivan (n.d.), "Drowning in big data? Reducing information technology complexities and costs for healthcare organizations." [online]. Available at www.emc.com/collateral/analyst-reports/frost-sullivan-reducing-information-technology-complexities-ar.pdf [Accessed January 2, 2018].

10 Frost and Sullivan (n.d.), "Drowning in big data? Reducing information technology complexities and costs for healthcare organizations." [online]. Available at www.emc.com/collateral/analyst-reports/frost-sullivan-reducing-information-technology-complexities-ar.pdf [Accessed January 2, 2018].

11 Knowledgent (2013), "Big data and healthcare payers." [online]. Available at https://knowledgent.com/whitepaper/big-data-and-healthcare-payers/ [Accessed January 23, 2018].

12 Institute for Health Technology Transformation (2013), "Transforming health care through big data strategies for leveraging big data in the health care industry." [online]. Available at http://c4fd63cb482ce6861463-bc6183f1c18e748a49b87a25911a0555.r93.cf2.rackcdn.com/iHT2_BigData_2013.pdf [Accessed January 23, 2018].

13 Capgemini (2012), "The deciding factor: Big data & decision making." [online]. Available at https://www.capgemini.com/resources/the-deciding-factor-big-data-decision-making/ [Accessed January 23, 2018].

14 S. Connolly and S. Wooledge (2013), "Harnessing the value of big data analytics." Hortonworks.

15 Intel (2012), "Big data analytics."

16 B. Feldman, E.M. Martin and T. Skotnes (2012), "Big data in healthcare hype and hope." *Dr. Bonnie 360.*

17 Institute for Health Technology Transformation (2013), "Transforming health care through big data strategies for leveraging big data in the health care industry." [online]. Available at http://c4fd63cb482ce6861463-bc6183f1c18e748a49b87a25911a0555.r93.cf2.rackcdn.com/iHT2_BigData_2013.pdf [Accessed January 23, 2018].

18 F. Ohlhorst (2012), *Big Data Analytics: Turning Big Data into Big Money.* New York: John Wiley & Sons.

19 D. Bollier (2010), *The Promise and Peril of Big Data.* Washington, DC: The Aspen Institute.

20 Institute for Health Technology Transformation (2013), "Transforming health care through big data strategies for leveraging big data in the health care industry." [online]. Available at http://c4fd63cb482ce6861463-bc6183f1c18e748a49b87a25911a0555.r93.cf2.rackcdn.com/iHT2_BigData_2013.pdf [Accessed January 23, 2018].

21 Dr. John Haughom, Senior Advisor, et al. (2017), "Health Catalyst: The changing role of healthcare data analysts—How our most successful clients are embracing healthcare transformation (executive report)." [online]. Available at https://www.healthcatalyst.com/the-changing-role-of-healthcare-data-analysts/ [Accessed January 23, 2018].

22 Jon Wettersten and Dean Malmgren (2018), "What happens when data scientists and designers work together." *Harvard Business Review.* [online]. Available at https://hbr.org/2018/03/what-happens-when-data-scientists-and-designers-work-together [Accessed March 29, 2018].

23 Leandro DalleMule and Thomas H. Davenport (2017), "What's your data strategy?" *Harvard Business Review,* May–June, 112–121.

How to ignite adoption and diffusion of new digital tools **6**

Adoption and diffusion are probably more important than new tools development aspects of technological innovation because that's where the "donkey falls"—so to speak—and any innovation that doesn't plan for adoption and diffusion is on the right road to failure even if the technology itself is outstanding. In this chapter, after introducing the innovation process, we will explore the methods/tools to build successful adoption and diffusion among both physicians and consumers/patients.

We'll begin our journey with a **leading case history** on igniting adoption and diffusion of new digital tools in action at Concord Hospital, a 230-bed community hospital in New Hampshire.[1] The secret to Concord's success is its commitment to investing in HIT adoption to improve care delivery.

As Concord Hospital transitioned to Computerized Physician Order Entry (CPOE), the HIT project team which includes Dr. Joel Berman (chief medical information officer), Dr. David Green (chief medical officer), Dean Morrison (chief information officer) and physician informaticists Dr. Paul Clark, Dr. Wendy Angelo, and Dr. David Picard, created a methodology that set users (primarily physicians) up to succeed.

The team worked one department at a time to prototype workflow processes and to develop forms that reflected the way that physicians thought and cared for patients.

The goal was to meet the "five rights" of technology—the right information at the right time to the right person in the right format and the right medium.

1. *Right information* is specific to the patient and actionable at the point of care.
2. *Right time* focuses on presenting clinical decision support at the moment most congruent with the clinician's workflow; for example, a prompt about the need for an echocardiogram should be given when the provider is thinking about cardiovascular orders.
3. *Right person* addresses issues such as, "Should a prompt about undocumented smoking status go to a physician, nurse or medical assistant?"
4. *Right format* refers to the interface properties within a specific medium; for example, within CPOE, a prompt should come up about a CMS (Center for Medicare & Medicaid Services) core indicator with passive text guidance, an intrusive pop-up or a mandatory hard stop.
5. *Right medium* specifies the application used to deliver the clinical decision support; examples of a decision support medium include the CPOE, physician portal, intranet or a third-party resource such as UpToDate or Micromedex.

Concentrating on one department at a time allowed for rapid turnaround on clinical suggestions, promoted the perception that the team is listening to users, and minimized us-versus-them interactions between physicians and the team. Creating a supportive culture was important because the success of the project depended on dotted-line influence rather than top-down mandates.

Physician champions, as discussed in Cohn (2009), played an integral role in the design and implementation of the CPOE system and subsequent HIT projects at the hospital. Their involvement unfolds as follows:

• Seven additional physician champions from a variety of fields were enlisted in addition to the veteran physicians on the team. These physicians, all of whom are well respected by colleagues, helped build consensus on clinical processes and order sets.
• Two cardiologists lent their illegible orders to a "Stump the Staff" exercise to illustrate that illegible handwriting caused confusion and that a CPOE system is safer for patients.
• A general surgeon showed his surgical colleagues variation in their orders for vital signs, temperature elevation, low urine output, and incentive

spirometry as well as the consequences of the variation. His presentation demonstrated the need for consensus building and the benefits of standard-ization and led to a unified appendectomy order set.

• Physician champions in pediatrics, obstetrics, orthopedics and internal medicine also leveraged their credibility, communication skills and time.

Because physician champions are experts in the workflow critical to care delivery, their input increases the probability that the new care processes will be embraced by other clinicians and improve medical outcomes (see Opinion Leader Mapping and Management in Chapter 7).

The success of Concord Hospital's approach lays on the following main factors:

1. *Physician participation at the planning stage.* This very first step is critical to both the design and widespread use of the HIT project.
2. *Sufficient resources allocation.* The planning process also involved the alloca-tion of sufficient human and financial resources to the effort, including a group made up of 13 physicians and clinical staff members.
3. *Logical framework adoption.* The team used Kotter's (1996) 8-step change model as an implementation framework. One of the benefits of Kotter's model is that it urges teams to perform the ground work (steps 1 through 4, which Kotter referred to as "defrosting activities") first and then embed the change (step 8). In this way, the change is more likely to be sustainable. At Concord, Kotter's 8-step change model articulated as follows:

Step 1: *Create urgency for change.* The "Stump the Staff" exercise mentioned earlier revealed life-threatening dangers of paper-based orders. While the demonstration began humorously with bad handwriting samples, it led to a serious presentation of a case that involved an 18-month-old's nearly fatal overdose from an anti-seizure drug. The primary care practitioner who wrote the illegible order was a respected 26-year veteran of the medical staff, driv-ing home the point that medical errors are caused by bad systems, not bad doctors.

Step 2: *Pull together a guiding team.* As mentioned above, having a well-respected team to champion the process and align resources to achieve the objectives is critical to success.

Step 3: *Create a clear, uplifting vision.* For example, the team spelled out the CPOE vision using the easy-to-remember initials of the project:

a. C is for clinical decision support at the point of care. Order sets must be right for most patients most (80%) of the time.

b. P is for patient-centered care. Tools that customize care for the other 20% of orders must be tailored to individual needs, on the basis of patients' diseases, other medications, metabolism and preferences.

c. O is for ordering efficiency. Transmission of orders to the receiving department must be near instantaneous, when compared to paper-based orders.

d. E is for electronic database. The back-end clinical repository of orders and outcomes that the team analyzes must be informative so that improvements can continually be made to the C, P, and O components. This vision points out that CPOE is not an application but a transformative, iterative journey to improve patient care.

Step 4: *Communicate the message many times using multiple channels.* For example, the team presented "Stump the Staff" at grand rounds, medical staff quarterly meetings, and department meetings as well as to nurses, allied healthcare professionals, and other employees who could spread the word about the hospital's efforts.

Step 5: *Empower people by removing obstacles.* This step entailed establishing CPOE order sets (tools) and enlisting physician champions in each specialty. Doing so facilitated the use of the system and engaged users, thereby removing barriers to implementation. The team's message to physicians who opted not to use CPOE is consistent: "Don't use CPOE if you think it might compromise the care your patient receives, but please tell us why you chose not to use CPOE so that we can address the problem and improve it."

Step 6: *Create short-term wins that provide momentum.* At Concord, the Diabetes Physician Recognition Program bound physicians to the optimal way to care for patients with diabetes and heart disease and who suffered a stroke. Showing physicians a quality dashboard that displays how well/poorly their patients are doing compared with those of their colleagues and with national averages can trigger healthy competition (Cohn 2009).

Step 7: Maintain momentum so that wave after wave of change is possible.

Following improvements in the prophylaxis of patients with venous thromboembolism, for example, the team piloted an inpatient diabetes order set that in its early stages reduced hypoglycemic reactions by 67%, compared with results from previous diabetes management systems.

Step 8: *Make change stick by nurturing a new culture.* When the team embarked on establishing electronic tools (see step 5), the team invited physicians to get involved. As an enticement for participating in afterhours meetings, physicians were offered gift certificates to local stores.

Many physicians declined the gift certificates, stating that work to improve patient care did not require extra reimbursement. The team interpreted the physicians' response as a sign that it conducted the "defrosting activities" well.

Today, approximately 135,000 of the 150,000 patients served by Concord Hospital have electronic health records, and 95% of Concord physicians use the EMR system. In addition, Concord has helped three other hospitals in the area with technology adoption (Rhea 2009).[2]

You are not getting too far without an *effective implementation*, though!

Overall, implementing new technology throughout the organization is inherently disruptive, especially in healthcare where patient care cannot cease to make way for the unfettered installation of a new system. Often, parallel systems must run to accommodate the transition, despite the additional burdens and workflow challenges it places on healthcare staff (Chaiken 2008a).[3]

The ideal way to implement HIT is to pay attention to the details before the implementation, including the following:

- *Selecting a HIT system.* The clinical strategic vision of the organization must drive the HIT system purchase. A poorly chosen system can lead physicians to move their practice to competing facilities, disrupt patient care and usher in lawsuits. The purchase decision must be based on surrogate information, such as the system's clinical decision support feature, other organizations' and users' satisfaction with the system, and perceived relevance and ease of use of the system's applications. The safest way to evaluate an installed HIT system is to visit the current clients of each vendor to observe the system's functioning in various patient care areas and at peak usage times. Selecting a HIT system requires patience and time.
- *Forging a vendor relationship.* An outstanding working relationship with a system vendor may trump the minor upgrades in features and functionality of another system that offers suboptimal customer support. A vendor relationship extends far beyond the adoption and implementation phase, so it is important *to partner* with a trustworthy vendor who can offer guarantees that the system will deliver expected results long after the purchase. Because unexpected problems will arise, a positive vendor relationship can ensure that problems are resolved immediately and support is available at all times.
- *Negotiating prices.* The products, services and support included in the system's price should be scrutinized during the negotiation with the vendor. Cost of ownership includes not only the purchase price but also ongoing maintenance, support and upgrades.

- *Preparing physicians for implementation.* Following a method recommended by Kenneth H. Cohn et al. (2009) for preparing the medical staff for HIT implementation.
    1. Convene a panel (6–10 members) of physicians who have clinical credibility and who represent various disciplines.
    2. Ask the panel to discuss with their colleagues the features and traits of a HIT system that are most important to their work. Panel members should encourage physicians to talk to peers at other organizations that have rolled out a HIT project.
    3. Invite vendors to submit a proposal and perform a demonstration for the panel and the medical staff.
    4. Use a scoring system to evaluate the HIT system according to features, reliability, training, service, upgrades and cost.
    5. Visit organizations that are using the top five systems as presented by the vendors. Visit at peak hours and talk with users about the system's strengths and weaknesses.
    6. Request all departments to review their workflows and clinical processes to identify those that may be streamlined.
    7. Schedule meetings with physicians to discuss their concerns.
    8. Schedule meetings with nursing, pharmacy, laboratory and other allied departments to discuss their concerns.
    9. If necessary, hire a consultant to help evaluate different vendors; systems; pricing; features; and time frames for installation, training, assistance and repairs.
    10. Designate internal trainers and ensure that the selected vendor provides them with comprehensive training. These internal trainers will serve as a resource for physicians and staff during implementation.
    11. Provide mandatory training sessions for physicians and their assistants/support staff. Trained physician users become invaluable champions of the HIT effort (Chaiken 2008b).[4]
- *Planning the "go-live" date and beyond.* Plans must be in place for the date that the system is scheduled to begin operating and beyond that date.
    1. Minimize elective clinical procedures for one month after the go-live date to accommodate initial system inefficiencies.
    2. Install vendor representatives and internal trainers on patient care floors for at least the first week after the go-live date.
    3. Offer refresher courses periodically or advanced sessions monthly/ quarterly after the system is in place.

4. Compile frequently asked questions and answers in a web-based data repository (wiki media) to facilitate training of new physicians and clinical staff.
5. Track quality and safety metrics, billing accuracy, adoption and user satisfaction before and after implementation. Then, display these data on a dashboard and distribute them for monthly review to physicians, organizational leaders and board members.

Key learnings

- Physician engagement is the primary determinant of HIT implementation success.
- Unintended problems and consequences will arise. Do not expect any system to work as advertised by the vendor.
- Consensus building is essential not only to HIT implementation but also to establishing improved clinical processes and outcomes.

The success of HIT adoption and implementation are as much a matter of organizational culture as engineering design. Successful healthcare organizations such as Concord Hospital can reap gains in quality, safety and coordination of care by welcoming innovation, rather than view it as a threat.

In addition, for healthcare institutions and medical practices, successful patient empowerment relies not just on new technology but also on a cultural shift. As the industry adapts to these changes, providers and healthcare administration must be prepared to face obstacles such as:

- difficulty shifting behaviors;
- different communication preferences;
- lack of health information exchanges;
- technology ease of use operational and implementation challenges workforce reluctance.

As already highlighted, the many benefits of new healthcare technology and patient empowerment have been proven to outweigh the costs and challenges of implementation. However, successful adaptation and cultural shifts rarely occur without obstacles. Also, one of the biggest challenges that remain is the implementation of effective evidence-based methods of measurement for patient engagement (we'll explore this topic in Chapter 9). In this Chapter we'll focus specifically on adoption and diffusion.

The innovation process

Before focusing on adoption and diffusion let's give a quick look at the definition of innovation and innovation process (including ideation).

Firstly, before embarking on a journey to bring your ideas to life, it is important to make the distinction between an invention and innovation. An invention is creating something new that the market has not seen before. An innovation is taking an existing concept or idea and improving it, typically using a step-wise process of developmental stages leading to a commercially viable product.

The innovation process includes the following steps:

Step 1—Identifying the goals or problems to be solved: Clarify what your business's innovation goals are and why you want, or need to engage in this kind of innovation. It is important to involve a good cross-section of the business in developing these goals, utilizing the expertise within the organization including physicians patients and any other stakeholder influenced and influencing the adoption and diffusion of your innovation.

Step 2—Analysis: Some real-world discovery of the current situation, customers, their needs, challenges, etc. In addition to customers, it is vital to look into what the competition is doing, any trends which will impact on your business, and which innovations organizations outside your industry are implementing that you can learn from. You should check inside your own organization to determine what assets, resources and core competencies you have within your company that you can apply.

Step 3—Development and design: Based on the information and thoughts gained during analysis, it is advisable to develop an ideas portfolio that includes ways you could innovate to meet these goals and problems. Once you have developed these ideas, an initial evaluation and prioritization will lead to a portfolio of innovations you can test.

Step 4—Conversion: Translate the ideas into practical innovation products and/or initiatives that could be targeted toward the identified audience. The aim here is not to fully launch the innovative products and/or initiatives but to test your ideas within a limited scope to determine whether customers like the innovation, accept it and are willing to adopt it/pay. This means providing prototypes complete with some basis of costing and a rudimentary process to make or design them.

This is a very important step, as innovations will probably have to be modified and changed in the light of customer or market feedback. During this part of the work the importance of protecting your intellectual property is critical.

Step 5—Introduction/Commercialization: The final step is where you take tested innovations and develop them to full-scale operations.

Innovation requires the careful balancing of risk and reward at all stages and will be influenced by the organizations culture and view on when, and with whom to share this.

The psychology of innovations

The marketplace performance of an innovation principally involves[5] three interrelated factors—the innovation itself, the firm doing the innovating and the consumers doing the adoption. These entities can be viewed as three points in an equilateral triangle, as reflected in Figure 6.1. At the center of this triangle one can place the economic utility or objective value of the innovation, which should determine the appeal of the product to both the firm and the consumer. One can think of this as a "rational framework" for understanding the market appeal of an innovation.

Gourville (2005) argues that perceptions about an innovation's value, on the part of both the consumer and the firm, render this rational model incomplete and inaccurate. Specifically, the perceived value of an innovation will be systematically and significantly impacted by the behavior change inherent in that innovation. The result is the modified "behavioral framework" presented in Figure 6.2 with economic utility replaced by perceived value. There are three essential components to this framework—the behavior change inherent in the innovation (A), the consumer's valuation of the innovation in light of that behavior change (B), and a firm's valuation of the innovation in light of the change (C).

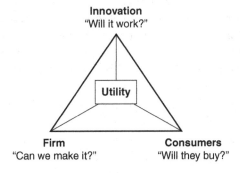

Figure 6.1 A rational framework for thinking about the marketing of innovations

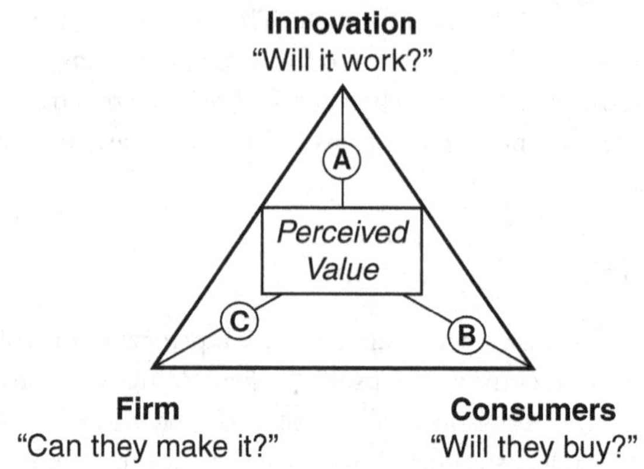

Innovation
"Will it work?"

(A)

Perceived Value

(C)   (B)

Firm   **Consumers**
"Can they make it?"   "Will they buy?"

Figure 6.2 A behavioral framework for thinking about the marketing of innovations

Briefly, the dynamics are as follows. Innovations often demand behavior change—i.e. consumers must give up one way of doing things and adopt a new, presumably better, way of doing things. But consumers tend to psychologically overweight that which they are being asked to give up (e.g. the benefits of the current alternative) relative to what they can get (e.g., the benefits of the innovation). In contrast, developers tend to psychologically overweight the benefits of their innovation relative to the benefits of the current alternative. The result is a clash in perspectives, one in which developers, who psychologically overvalue their innovation are predicting the likely actions of consumers, who psychologically overvalue the existing technology. As a result, consumers often reject innovations that would make them better off and developers often are at a loss to anticipate this rejection, thereby increasing the probability of market failure for the innovation. I call this the "curse of innovation."[6]

So what is a firm to do? The first step is to ask, "How much change are you asking of customers?" In particular what losses are you asking them to incur, both in the form of new costs (of money, time or effort) and foregone benefits. Therein lie both the opportunity and the dilemma facing the developers of innovations. Innovations create value through product change. As reflected in Figure 6.3, it is these product changes that create real value. The greater the technological change, the greater the potential for a breakthrough product. But product change often necessitates behavioral change. How we refuel our car, how we develop our pictures and how we think about "spare change" all change. While product change is often necessary for value creation, minimizing behavioral change helps to capture that value.

Methods and tools to build successful adoption and diffusion among both physicians and consumers/patients

The diffusion of innovation is the process by which new products are adopted (or not) by their intended audiences. The process can be used to evaluate the efficiency of an adoption strategy and thus examine how that strategy can be amended to improve adoption. The idea of diffusion was originally explored by Gabriel Tarde, a French sociologist, in the nineteenth century. One of the most significant early studies was conducted by Ryan and Gross in 1943. In his book *Diffusion of Innovations*, published in 1962, Everett Rogers, a sociology professor, provides a full framework for diffusion of innovation based on over 500 studies into the phenomenon in many different disciplines.[7]

The process for diffusion of innovation

As anticipated in Chapter 3, Rogers draws on Ryan and Gross's work to deliver a five-stage process for the diffusion of innovation which includes:

1. *Knowledge:* At this stage the would-be adopters are first exposed to the innovation itself. They do not have enough information to make a decision to purchase on and have not yet been sufficiently inspired to find out more. Marketers will need to increase awareness of the product and provide enough education that the prospective adopter moves to the second stage.
2. *Persuasion:* The prospective adopters are open to the idea of purchase. They are actively seeking information which will inform their eventual decision. Marketers will be seeking to convey the benefits of the product in detail.
3. *Decision:* Eventually the would-be adopters must make a decision. They will weigh up the pros and cons of adoption and either accept the innovation or reject it. Rogers cites this as the most difficult phase on which to acquire intelligence due, at least in part, to the fact that people do not make rational decisions in many instances. They make a decision based on their underlying perceptions and feelings and following the decision they attempt to rationalize that decision (we'll see more about this in the next paragraph).
4. *Implementation:* Once a decision to adopt a product has been made the product will, in most cases, be used by the purchaser. This stage is when the adopter makes a decision as to whether or not the product is actually useful to them. They may also seek out further information to either support the

use of the product or to better understand the product in context. This phase is interesting because it suggests that designers and marketers alike need to consider the ownership process in detail. How can a user obtain useful information in the post-sale/post-introduction environment? The quality of the implementation experience is going to be determined, to a lesser or greater extent, by the ease of access to information and the quality of that information.

5. *Confirmation:* This is the point at which the user evaluates their decision and decides whether they will keep using the product or abandon use of the product. This phase can only be ended by abandonment of a product otherwise it is continual.

The involvement of an individual at stages of the adoption process includes the following steps which are to be considered in relation to the decision steps in order to decide which actions to take to ignite adoption (Figure 6.1 above):

1. *Awareness:* The primary function is to initiate the sequence of later stages that lead to eventual adoption or rejection of the innovation.' This stage is described as a relatively passive one on the part of the receiver; he/she feels that awareness of an innovation does not generally come about as a result of a need, but rather that awareness of a new idea creates a need for that innovation.

2. *Interest:* The function of the interest stage is mainly to increase the individual's information about the innovation. We might speculate that the less information-seeking required, the more readily will the innovation be accepted. However ... as the individual's behavior becomes more purposive in seeking information, his psychological involvement increases. We may conclude, therefore, that the active seeking of information implies some degree of personal commitment, and may presage later phases more likely to result in adoption.

3. *Evaluation:* This stage is a "period of 'mental trial' which is a necessary preliminary to the decision to make a 'behavioral trial.'" At the evaluation stage the individual mentally applies the innovation to his present and anticipated future situation, and then decides whether or not to try it. This stage is considered to be the least defined of the five stages, which, therein creates the most difficulty in information gathering. Different types of evaluation occur at each stage in the adoption process ... but the decision to try the new idea occurs, by definition, only at the evaluation stage.

4. *Trial:* If the results of the individual's "mental trial" are favorable, he/she is ready to move on to the Trial stage. At the trial stage the individual uses the innovation on a small scale in order to determine its utility in his

ADOPTION PROCESS	DECISION PROCESS
Awareness	Knowledge
Interest	Persuasion
Evaluation	Decision
Trial	Implementation
Adoption	Confirmation

Figure 6.3 Relation between adoption and decision process

own situation. The main function of the trial stage is to demonstrate the new idea in the individual's own situation and determine its usefulness for possible complete adoption. It is not possible, of course, to try out all innovations on a small scale. An alternative in some cases is to make a trial on a temporary or probationary basis before going on to true adoption.

5. *Adoption:* It is at this stage that the results of the trial are considered, and on the basis of this the decision is made to adopt (or reject) the innovation.

It is worth noting that while adoption is the process by which a user begins and continues to use a product, diffusion is a measure of the rate of adoption. It considers the relationship not just between any given user and a product but the relationship between all users, each other and the product.

Rogers' diffusion studies offered some interesting advice for driving the rate of diffusion including:

- Examining social networks (it's worth noting that Rogers wasn't talking about Facebook or LinkedIn here, though the idea applies in a similar way in digital networks but rather "real life" social networks) and finding highly respected individuals and working with them to create desire for an innovation.
- Determining a representative group of desired users and "injecting" the innovation into that group to gain positive feedback, case studies, etc., to help make the decision-making process easier for other would-be early adopters.

Diffusion recognizes that adoption is not an isolated process but rather one which is influenced heavily by other members of the adoption cycle.

The diffusion of adoption is important to marketers and designers because it considers adoption in context of a larger social system. The aim is not just to support an individual through the adoption process but rather a community through that process. Understanding each step in the diffusion of adoption allows you to creatively examine how you might influence people at each stage—including the final stage of confirmation where a user may begin to influence others in their purchasing decisions too.

The impact of Rogers' characteristics on consumer adoption of an innovation can be considered in terms of:

Relative advantage—is the "the degree to which the innovation is perceived as better than the idea it supersedes. Relative advantage refers to the extent to which the innovation is more productive, efficient, costs less, or improves in some other manner upon existing practices."

Compatibility—is "the degree to which the innovation is perceived as being consistent with existing values, past experiences, and needs of potential adopters ... An innovation must be considered socially acceptable to be implemented. And some innovations require much time and discussion before they become socially acceptable."

Complexity (simplicity)—is "the degree to which the innovation is perceived as difficult to understand and use."

Observability—is "the degree to which the results of the innovation are visible to others. The chances of adoption are greater if folks can easily observe relative advantages of the new technology. In fact, after some adopt, observability can improve the diffusion effect, a critical component of technology transfer."

Trialability—is "the degree to which the innovation may be experimented with on a limited basis. Innovations are easier to adopt if they can be tried out in part, on a temporary basis, or easily dispensed with after trial."

In general, innovations that are perceived as having relative advantages, being more compatible, less complex, observable and *trialable* will diffuse more rapidly than other innovations.

Rogers identifies the following main categories of consumers (Figure 6.4):

1. *Innovators (risk takers)*—are the first individuals to adopt an innovation. They are willing to take risks.
2. *Early adopters (hedgers)*—are the second fastest category to adopt an innovation.
3. *Early majority (waiters)*—the third group, tends to take more time to consider adopting new innovations and is inclined to draw from feedback from early adopters before taking the risk of purchasing new products/systems.
4. *Late majority (skeptics)*—adopts the innovation after it has been established in the marketplace and is seldom willing to take risks with new innovation.
5. *Laggards (slow pokes)*—are the last to adopt an innovation. They tend to prefer traditions and are unwilling to take risks.

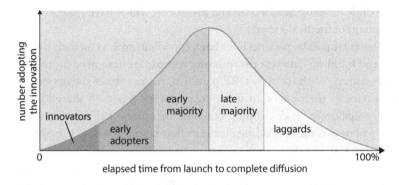

Figure 6.4 Rogers' main categories of consumers

Empowering physicians and patients with crowdsourcing and co-creation

Organizations who are listening and involving physicians and patients in decision-making are becoming popular and better liked by them. Leveraging the internal collaboration programs with external communication planning has an impact on the overall new technology perception and/or the expected result.

A crowdsourcing or co-creation project may become an "innovative" way to engage patients and generate change while promoting the adoption and diffusion of new digital tools.

A leading positive example is AMA's Physician Innovation Network. In October 2017, the American Medical Association (AMA) introduced an online physician community where doctors can connect with companies and entrepreneurs who are looking for physician input in the development of healthcare technology products and services.[8] The goal is to help improve new products while they are in development.

The Physician Innovation Network provides an open online forum for physicians to explore paid and volunteer opportunities to collaborate with health tech companies and for entrepreneurs to search for physicians with the expertise they need. The platform also provides both physicians and health tech entrepreneurs with opportunities to learn from like-minded innovators and medical professionals, including access to virtual panel discussions with experts.

Another interesting case history about crowdsourcing in action is PatientsLikeMe, the Cambridge, MA-based company, a provider of patient social networking communities, that received grants totaling $4.3 million from the Robert Wood Johnson Foundation to lead an effort that puts patients at the center of developing health outcome measures, which have traditionally been the domain of medical experts.

At PatientsLikeMe, patients have been contributing data on their diseases for years and building data sets that pharma companies have used to inform their drug research. With the new ORE platform, patients have the opportunity to offer advice to their peers, to foster relationships based on shared attributes, and to collaborate on developing outcome measures that better evaluate the efficacy of new drugs, including elements that matter to those taking the medicines, that is patients.

Besides AMA and PatientsLikeMe, some other interesting and groundbreaking healthcare organizations are already using crowdsourcing to innovatively engage their patients and enhance their experience:[9]

- CrowdMed charges patients a $199 fee to share their disease experience and obtain a probable diagnosis from the crowd of MDs ("medical detectives" in this case). Almost 3,000 MDs (doctors and residents) have registered as medical detectives.
- Webicina is a site where medicine combines with social media to allow physicians across the world to communicate their findings easily, quickly, and effectively.
- Biopharma company UCB partnered with PatientsLikeMe to create an online, open epilepsy community that captures real-world experiences of people living with epilepsy in the US. Launched in early 2010, this platform is designed to collect, analyze and reflect information received from people with epilepsy, regardless of their diagnosis, prognosis, or treatment regimen (Brodie, 2002).[10]
- CureTogether is a social health collaborative that brings patients with hundreds of conditions together in overlapping data communities. CureTogether was launched in July 2008 by Alexandra Carmichael and Daniel Reda to help the people they knew and the millions they didn't who live in daily chronic pain. Starting with three conditions, it quickly expanded as people wrote in to request that their conditions be added to this ongoing study. CureTogether is a social business, currently funded by its founders and angel investment, and has partnered with several universities and research organizations.[11]
- GE partnered with Kaggle to launch crowdsourced "Quests." The hospital quest is an open call for application ideas that will incorporate operational solutions "that can promote an improved healthcare system experience for patient and family." The hospital competition features a judges' panel, made up of representatives from GE, Ochsner Health System, and Kaggle.

They will be evaluating ideas on their overall quality, potential impact, and ease of adoption and implementation. While medicine should be left to the professionals, many aspects of hospital operations are ripe for rethinking. In this Quest, focus on operational (non-medical) solutions that can promote an improved healthcare system experience for patient and family.[12]

Likewise, some interesting and ground-breaking healthcare organizations are already using co-creation to innovatively communicate with their patients and enhance their experience.

- TickiT. A collaborative industry and academic partnership with the Emily Carr University of Art and Design (ECUAD) conducted the co-creation process aiming at leveraging youth's comfort with technology to develop TickiT, a youth-friendly interactive mobile eHealth psychosocial screening tool. Whitehouse et al. (2013) chose to use co-creation processes and methods with the goal of increasing patient engagement and simplifying HCP work, thereby improving patient/provider communication and experience while meeting regulatory requirements. Here co-creation process differs from the traditional method of involving passive stakeholders during the latter phase of prototype testing. Instead, it views them as active contributors with knowledge and skills for co-creation during the ideation phase.[13]
- Flamingo and Epic Pharmacy Healthcare Co-Creation Partnership. The Flamingo platform launched in 2014 supports a new and innovative approach to customer relationships and retention. Flamingo is a leading Australian software developer while Epic Pharmacy (EPIC), is one of Australia's largest, specialty pharmacy groups providing hospital, oncology, and aged-care pharmacy services. This innovative platform enables customers to co-create their desired experience by personalizing the way they communicate, how they interact with and want to be treated by an organization, and the mix of goods or services they want to receive.[14]

Introducing evidence-based digital tools

The health and technology communities have been buzzing about the possibilities of digital health, but is it possible those boosters have argued beyond the evidence? The clinical proof underpinning the effectiveness of digital health is, so far, somewhat sparse.

Between the government's electronic health record incentive programs pumping billions into healthcare, and private sector interest, investment in the sector is rising. But what if the evidence doesn't support that enthusiasm?

1a. The home screen of *In Hand* – users are presented with this screen when *In Hand* is opened.

1b. Example of a screen that is presented if user clicks 'Great' on the home screen.

1c. Example of a screen that is presented if user clicks 'So-So' on the home screen.

1d. The screen that is presented if user clicks 'Not Good' on the home screen. The options here link to other functions on the user's smartphone.

1e. The screen that is presented if user clicks 'Awful' on the home screen. The third option ('Sue Radford' in above screenshot) is an example of the 'Someone To Call' option being used.

Figure 6.5 Screenshots and description of *In Hand* app

We will explore what are the expected digital health's benefits and how to design and introduce evidence-based tools by analyzing a leading case history on evaluation of digital technologies in action conducted by E.B. Davies, M.P. Craven, J.L. Martin et al. (2017) for *In Hand* (www.inhand.org.uk, launched 2014), a mental well-being smartphone app developed by young people with experience of mental health problems to support well-being through focusing the user on the current moment and bringing balance to everyday life. *In Hand* is a simple, free-to-download digital self-help tool publicly available on iOS and Android, intended to be used independently of healthcare services. Using a traffic-light-inspired system, the app takes the user through different activities depending on how they are feeling (see Figure 6.5).[15] Its development was led by a UK arts organization, working with a digital agency and a public mental health service provider. The project's clinical lead drew on principles of cognitive behavior therapy and Five Ways to Well-being[10] during the development process, but the primary influence on the content arose from needs derived in the co-design process that explored coping strategies used by young people at times of stress or low mood.

NIHR MindTech HTC was commissioned to undertake an independent evaluation of a suite of digital resources produced by Innovation Labs;[11] *In Hand* was one of these products. As these digital resources were about to be publicly launched as the evaluation stage commenced, the team proposed to observe how users engaged with the tools by capturing background usage data and seeking feedback directly from users through embedding user elicitation into the tools. This approach would enable the capture of insights from naturally occurring users and gain understanding of how people interact with it in the "real world."

Three methods of data collection were used to gain insight into naturalistic use of *In Hand*: (1) sampling and analysis of quantitative mobile analytical data (i.e. number of individual user sessions, number of interactions with each section of the app); (2) a user survey with questions adapted from a validated well-being measure (the Short Warwick-Edinburgh Mental Well-being Scale[16] (SWEMWBS)) and (3) semi-structured individual interviews with a subsample of survey respondents.

The *user survey* and semi-structured interview topic guide were developed specifically for this study. Young people involved with Innovation Labs and *In Hand* development collaborated with the National Institute for Health Research (NIHR)MindTech Team[17] in generating the study's design and areas to be explored in the survey and interview, reviewing and testing out the online survey and interview schedule and finalizing the study materials. To explore the kinds of benefits *In Hand* had to users, the survey questions were based on the SWEMWBS,[18] an evidence-based measurement tool with seven dimensions of mental well-being which has been shown to be valid and reliable with young people.[19] In this real world, observational evaluation, it was not possible to assess participants' well-being before and after use of the app, but rather users were asked to rate to what extent *In Hand* had helped them on specific dimensions of mental well-being. During the co-design process, one of these dimensions was reworded to be more accessible to young people ("feel optimistic" changed to "have a positive outlook"), and three other dimensions were selected for inclusion in the survey to reflect the young people's experiences ("feel ready to talk to someone else," "feel less stressed," "feel more able to take control"). These dimensions were also used to guide the interview topics.

Aggregated analytical data from Flurry Analytics (a tool that captures usage data for smartphone/tablet apps) were tabulated and summary statistics calculated. To assess users' engagement, the *In Hand* team were asked to advise on the time a user would need to spend on the app to have a "meaningful engagement": that is, open the app, make a selection of how they were feeling and perform at least one activity based on their response to the front screen (i.e., take a photo). Flurry gives data on session length in fixed ranges (see Table 6.1). It was likely that many sessions recorded as less than 30 s would have been too short for the user to have completed an activity. Therefore, user sessions in the range 30–60 s and above were classed as "meaningful engagement."

From launch of *In Hand* on May 14 to October 31, 2014, there were 22,357 user sessions on *In Hand* across both mobile platforms (14,981 on iPhone; 7,376 on Android). Seventy-five percent of these were returning users. Sixteen percent remained active 1 week after first use (likely to be at installation), 7% after 4 weeks and 2% after 20 weeks. Around half of the users (52%) opened *In Hand*

Table 6.1 Time spent on *In Hand* at each user session

Length of time for each user session	Number of sessions, n (%)
0–3 s	2188 (10.9)
3–10 s	2230 (11.1)
10–30 s	3993 (19.8)
30–60 s	4185 (20.8)
1–3 min	5621 (27.9)
3–10 min	1717 (8.5)
10–30 min	213 (1.1)
30+min	10 (0.1)

once a week, with 34% using it 2–3 times per week, 10% 4–6 times and 4% more than 6 times per week.

Table 6.1 shows engagement with *In Hand* measured by the length of time of each user session (data were provided by the analytics in the ranges shown). More than half of users' sessions (58%) were in the "meaningful engagement" ranges of 30–60 s or longer and a further fifth of sessions (20%) were somewhere in the range of 10–30 s where some users may have had time to have meaningful engagement. Around a fifth (22%) were in the lower ranges of 10 s or less session length. Less than 10% of sessions were in a range over 3 min. Overall, the median session duration was 43 s for iPhone users and 40 s for Android users (Flurry reports the average as the median, rather than the mean).

The opening screen of *In Hand* presents the question "Hello, how are you feeling?" with four options: "Great," "So-So," "Not Good" and "Awful" and associated sub options (see Figure 9.1). The most frequent selection on this opening screen was "So-So" (11 751 occurrences), followed by "Not Good" (9,958 occurrences), "Great" (9,048 occurrences) and "Awful" (8,614 occurrences). In general, it was seen that users accessed the entire set of sub options but with some obvious preferences based on which of the four options they chose, for example, reading multiple inspirational quotes, viewing a personally loaded photo or using the "Jot it down" function (akin to a journal where users could type their thoughts into the app).

Table 6.2 summarizes how survey respondents reported *In Hand* helped their mental well-being. The ten mental well-being dimensions, including the seven from the SWEMWBS, are presented in rank order. For seven dimensions, over 60% of the survey respondents reported that *In Hand* had offered them some help, with three dimensions reported as being helpful by half or less of the respondents. For four dimensions, almost three-quarters (74%) or more reported *In Hand* was helpful to them—"More able to take control," "Think clearly," "Feel relaxed" and "Deal with problems well." These top four dimensions relate most closely

Table 6.2 Participants ratings of whether *In Hand* helped with their mental well-being (n=108), ranked in order by numbers endorsing it helped "a lot"

Would you say In Hand has helped you...	No way, n (%)	Not really, n (%)	Yes, a little bit, n (%)	Yes, a lot, n (%)
More able to take control	4 (3.7)	28 (25.9)	43 (39.8)	33 (30.6)
Think clearly*	3 (2.8)	25 (23.1)	51 (47.2)	29 (26.9)
Feel relaxed*	2 (1.9)	23 (21.3)	58 (53.7)	25 (23.1)
Deal with problems well*	5 (4.6)	37 (34.3)	41 (38.0)	25 (23.1)
Less stressed	4 (3.7)	20 (18.5)	60 (55.6)	24 (22.2)
Make my own mind up about things*	6 (5.6)	34 (31.5)	47 (43.5)	21 (19.4)
Have a positive outlook*	3 (2.8)	17 (15.7)	68 (63.0)	20 (18.5)
Feel useful*	5 (4.6)	39 (36.1)	49 (45.4)	15 (13.9)
Ready to talk to someone else	15 (13.9)	38 (35.2)	41 (38.0)	14 (13.0)
Feel close to other people*	18 (16.7)	43 (29.0)	29 (26.9)	14 (13.0)

*These items are taken from the Short Warwick-Edinburgh Mental Well-being Scale.

to the primary purpose of *In Hand*. For all of the dimensions, most respondents reported that *In Hand* had helped them "a little bit," rather than "a lot."

The eight interviewed participants were mostly female (n=7), aged 16–44 years (mean 25±9 years), white (n=7) and had experience of mental health problems (n=7). Interviewees further highlighted how *In Hand* helped the dimensions of their mental well-being as revealed in the survey, including describing how it helped them to feel relaxed or less stressed:

> I can get a bit panicky quite quickly, so if I just stop and go on something like *In Hand*, the ease of using it and the colors and everything, sort of calms you and takes your mind off what you are feeling ... looking at a quote helps you to feel more calm and relaxed.
>
> (Interviewee 8)

Helped to think clearly and more able to take control:

> *In Hand* is nice, so simple and it's just common sense, the things it asks you about how you are feeling. But that then leads you on to thinking about a lot of things. So for me, it gives me more independence with my emotional well-being.
>
> (Interviewee 7)

And helped to facilitate a positive outlook:

> The little sayings like 'keep going' I found helpful because it's something a friend might say if they were supporting you and it makes you realize that you can't just give up.
>
> (Interviewee 3)

The interviewees further expanded on why *In Hand* was useful to them. They talked about *In Hand* being discreet, private and not requiring them to be in specific locations to access it. Interviewees described how the anonymity and perceived non-judgmental nature of a digital tool was important to them. It gave them the ability to think about how they were feeling at any time without having to involve other people:

> There's no-one to trust on your app—it's just asking you how you are feeling. There's no kind of come back or no-one's going to say anything back.
>
> (Interviewee 1)

Key benefits of the evaluation approach

1. The evidence generated by this approach, which goes beyond user ratings in app stores, while being timely and cost-efficient to implement informed by the principles of Health Technology Assessment, has provided quantifiable insights into the app usage and patterns of engagement, an assessment of how the app has supported users with their mental wellbeing and identified some descriptive insights to how the tool works to support users.

2. The approach was able to gather data from actual users of the tool in real-world settings. By accessing the analytical data of all users within a specified time period, researchers were able to analyze, in aggregate, how people used the tool and how this changed over time. This may be different (or similar) from how people interact with a tool within a controlled setting: digital interventions in formal trials tend to have greater adherence than naturalistic evaluations.[20] Moreover, the survey and interview respondents were people who had selected the tool independently from a range available (via the app stores) and used it in naturally occurring ways, rather than a sample of volunteers using the tool under experimental, controlled conditions.

3. The evaluation plan (along with the app) was guided by a team of young people and proved achievable within a timescale to fit with the development cycles of digital tools. Evaluation commenced at the end of beta testing when the app first became available from app stores; data and analysis were communicated to the development team for implementation at their 6-month review point. The co-design process assisted in ascertaining that the evaluation methods were understandable and used language and a design familiar to its target audience. The methods adopted did not require

extensive digital development—which would have been outside the resources of the development and evaluation teams—and good response rates were achieved. Nor did it require retention of participants over time to generate useful insights.

4. While the approach used could be criticized for inability to determine the extent to which any changes to mental health are attributable to using *In Hand*, researchers would argue that their approach was not intended to measure effect, but rather assess the type of impact *In Hand* may have on users' mental well-being. A measurement of the effect of *In Hand* and the resources this would require is, they would argue, out of proportion to the nature of the tool and anticipated effect on mental well-being. *In Hand* is a self-help tool, commensurate with other self-help tools, such as books or online information, rather than a clinical intervention, treatment or psychological therapy, and *In Hand* is not a medical device. As such the level of evidence required to provide assurances of quality should not be expected to be as extensive as would be required for clinical interventions or medical devices. In this regard, researchers believe the methods adopted—including a validated measure of mental well-being to explore the nature of the effect—were sufficient to demonstrate this and can be considered a strength of the approach used. This assertion is supported by data from an associated evaluation of another simple digital tool—DocReady (www.docready.org)—which used the same standardized measure in a similar manner.[21] This evaluation found that DocReady was reported as useful in different domains of mental well-being to *In Hand*: the top three rated domains were "Able to think clearly," "Ready to talk to someone else" and "More able to take control," which reflects how DocReady aimed to benefit its users through changing preparatory intentions and behavior in seeking out help from a GP. As with *In Hand*, most users rated the help as "a little bit" rather than "a lot," confirming that both these tools have a limited, specific effect and, as would be expected, one mHealth app would not provide all the functions required for overall mental health.[22]

Improvement areas of the evaluation approach

1. In common with other evaluation methods, the sample for the survey and interviews was reliant on people opting in to participate, so is a self-selecting sample. These people are those most likely to have a positive experience with the tool or those wanting to feedback their

dissatisfaction—the so-called "TripAdvisor effect"—and people who "fall in the middle" may not be providing feedback. Likewise, it may be that users who found benefits of using the tool were more likely to be those that have "stuck with" the tool over time. In addition, the sample is relatively homogeneous—predominantly white females (the target audience for *In Hand* was young people aged up to 25 years, so the limited age range was as to be expected). This gender difference is observed in other research of similar tools,[23,24,25] but whether this is a mHealth usage or research participation bias is not clear.

2. While responses to the survey were good and numbers exceeded our initial target (see Figure 3), this probably represents a small proportion of overall users: because usage of the app is recorded in user sessions, rather than individuals, it was not possible to accurately estimate the response rate to the survey.

3. Interest in taking part in the interviews was very limited. In the event, researchers interviewed all those that agreed and achieved only eight in total: this was lower than our target number and it was not possible to sample from the specified criteria of interest (i.e., gender, different experience with the tool). The interview findings are therefore to be interpreted with caution as they are based on a small number of experiences with a homogeneous sample. Users of other backgrounds and demographics may have different perspectives on *In Hand*.

4. The time period between users first interacting with *In Hand* and the completion of the survey was not recorded. Therefore, an assessment of the influence of recall bias on the reliability of the results is not possible. However, users would have accessed the survey through the hyperlinks within the app, so it is probable that they completed it during an app session.

5. The Flurry Analytics software is designed for developers, rather than a research tool, which brings limitations. In particular, data were aggregated into predefined numerical ranges which acted to limit the analysis. For example, Flurry categorizes each individual user session into time ranges, rather than providing the actual time spent on the app. The precise format of data returned by Flurry depended on the smartphone operating system and did not always align well between these. Moreover, it was not possible to track an individual user's interactions with the app over time, for example to assess how consistent the usage was. The importance of using a more sophisticated individualized metric combining different aspects of user engagement (an "App Engagement Index") is a current topic in the mHealth literature[26] which could be adopted in future research.

Clinical implications of the evaluation approach

Davies, Craven, Martin et al. have demonstrated how simple, self-help digital tools can be evaluated in a proportionate and practical way. Triangulating data sources provided an understanding of how *In Hand* was used and the ways it can support mental well-being. In particular, the survey of naturally occurring users provided insights into the value of the app from the user perspective, and in this case provided evidence of the app having the intended effect for users. This is important for healthcare decision-makers who need to be assured of the quality of an app before recommending to patients. In addition, analytical data provides evidence of how and when a tool is being used (or not), which enables health providers and commissioners to make a judgment on the value of a tool in order to ensure any cost is justified (not applicable for in this case as the tool is free to use). Furthermore, they have demonstrated cost-efficient, timely methods, which can be easily incorporated into digital tools, thus providing scope for audits and service evaluations.

There is no doubt that HIT will ultimately transform healthcare delivery, self-management education and behavior change interventions. Indeed, healthcare organizations tend to slow innovation due to required evidence of effectiveness, privacy requirements, fear of liability, integration into existing technology ecosystem and demands for a demonstrated return on investment. At the same time, consumer brands are entering the digital health arena and making big bets on direct-to-consumer approaches without proof of important or long-term impacts (think health monitoring devices for wellness and gamification with health focus). This leads to the proliferation of well-designed experiences that promise to improve health but may have minimal effect. At the same time, these well-designed experiences raise consumers' expectations for the look, feel and interaction of digital programs used within the context of a clinical relationship. So while consumer expectations escalate, healthcare providers slow down their pace of innovation and change. And this will increasingly impact consumer engagement, consumer satisfaction, and consumers' perception of value. To bridge the gap, healthcare organizations must start now with (1) pilots to learn about the unique impacts of digital health programs on their populations, and (2) road maps to scale digital health solutions over time. So rather than considering program or technology purchases, healthcare organizations should consider population partnerships with vendors who will start small and scale over time to impact population health.[27]

"Planning for adoption and diffusion is critical to designing and introducing evidence based tools."

Notes

1 Kenneth H. Cohn, MD (2009), "Engaging physicians to adopt healthcare information technology." *Journal of Healthcare Management*, 54(5) September/October.

2 S. Rhea (2009), "A head start in technology: Foundation of IT helped Michael Green increase efficacy and strategic use." *Modern Healthcare* 39(7), C4–C5.

3 B.P. Chaiken (2008a), "Healthcare IT Solutions." In *The Business of Healthcare*, edited by K.H. Cohn and D. Hough, 127–29. Westport, CT: Praeger.

4 B.P. Chaiken (2008b), "Strategies for success: Clinical HIT implementation." *Patient Safety and Quality Healthcare* 5(4), 28–31.

5 John T. Gourville (2005), "Marketing of innovations Module II: The psychology of innovations," Harvard Business School, publication date: Sep 16, 2005; revision date: Oct 3, 2005.

6 John T. Gourville (2003), "Why consumers don't buy: The psychology of new product adoption." Harvard Business School Background Note 504-056, November (revised April 2004.).

7 Everett Rogers (2003), *Diffusion of Innovations*, 5th edition. New York: Free Press.

8 Bernie Monegain (2017), "AMA platform to connect physicians and health technology developers Physician Innovation Network builds on AMA efforts already underway around patient-centered, evidence-based, interoperable and outcomes-focused care." Healthcare IT News. [online]. Available at www.healthcareitnews.com/news/ama-platform-connect-physicians-and-health-technology-developers. [Accessed March 16, 2018].

9 Beyond Bandwidth Level 3 Communication blog, 2013. "Not alone in a crowd: Crowd-sourcing for healthcare." Level 3 Editor, Level 3 Communication, LLC. [online]. Available at http://blog.level3.com/healthcare/not-alone-in-a-crowd-crowdsourcing-for-healthcare/ [Accessed November 25, 2014].

10 M.J. Brodie and P. Kwan (2002), "Staged approach to epilepsy management." *Neurology*, suppl. 5, p. 58.

11 CureTogether Blog (n.d.). [online]. Available at http://curetogether.com/blog/about/ [Accessed December 1, 2014].

12 Crowdsourcing.org, The industry website (n.d.), "GE partners with Kaggle, launches crowdsourced 'Quests'." [online]. Available at www.crowdsourcing.org/editorial/ge-partners-with-kaggle-launches-crowdsourced-quests/22206 [Accessed December 1, 2014].

13 S.R. Whitehouse et al. (2013), "Co-creation with TickiT: Designing and evaluating a clinical eHealth platform for youth." *Journal of Medical Internet Research Research Protocols*, 2(2), e42.

14 Flamingo (2014). "Epic Pharmacy injects $1.5 million into Flamingo Healthcare Co-Creation platform." [online]. Available at http://new.flamingo.io/press/epic-pharmacy-injects-1-5-million-flamingo-healthcare-co-creation-platform/ [Accessed December 31, 2014].

15 E.B. Davies, M.P. Craven, J.L. Martin et al. (2017), "Proportionate methods for evaluating a simple digital mental health tool." *Evidence-Based Mental Health*, 20, 112–117. [online]. Available at http://ebmh.bmj.com/content/ebmental/early/2017/10/09/eb-2017-102755.full.pdf [Accessed March 9, 2018].

16 S. Stewart-Brown, A. Tennant, R. Tennant et al. (2009), "Internal construct validity of the Warwick-Edinburgh Mental Well-being Scale (WEMWBS): A Rasch analysis using data from the Scottish Health Education Population Survey." *Health Qual Life Outcomes*, 7, 15.

17 NIHR MindTech MedTech Co-operative is a national center focusing on the development, adoption and evaluation of new technologies for mental healthcare and dementia. It was established in 2013 (formerly as a Healthcare Technology Co-operative and since January 2018 as a MedTech and In-vitro diagnostic Co-operative) and is funded by the National Institute for Healthcare Research. MindTech brings together healthcare professionals, researchers, industry and the public.

18 S. Stewart-Brown, A. Tennant, R. Tennant et al. (2009), "Internal construct validity of the Warwick-Edinburgh Mental Well-being Scale (WEMWBS): A Rasch analysis using data from the Scottish Health Education Population Survey." *Health Qual Life Outcomes*, 7,15.

19 A. Clarke, T. Friede, R. Putz et al. (2011), "Warwick-Edinburgh Mental Well-being Scale (WEMWBS): Validated for teenage school students in England and Scotland. A mixed methods assessment." *BMC Public Health*, 11, 487.

20 H. Christensen, K.M. Griffiths and L. Farrer (2009), "Adherence in internet interventions for anxiety and depression." *J Med Internet Res*, 11, e13.

21 L. Simons, M. Craven and J. Martin (2015), *Learning from the Labs 2: Evaluating Effectiveness*. Nottingham: NIHR MindTech Healthcare Technology Co-operative.

22 N. Bidargaddi, P. Musiat, M. Winsall et al. (2017), "Efficacy of a web-based guided recommendation service for a curated list of readily available mental health and wellbeing mobile apps for young people: Randomized controlled trial." *J Med Internet Res*, 19, e141.

23 N. Bidargaddi, P. Musiat, M. Winsall et al. (2017), "Efficacy of a web-based guided recommendation service for a curated list of readily available mental health and wellbeing mobile apps for young people: Randomized controlled trial." *J Med Internet Res*, 19, e141.

24 R. Kenny, B. Dooley and A. Fitzgerald (2015), "Feasibility of "CopeSmart": A telemental health app for adolescents." *JMIR Ment Health*, 2, e22.

25 S.C. Reid, S.D. Kauer, S.J. Hearps et al. (2011), "A mobile phone application for the assessment and management of youth mental health problems in primary care: A randomized controlled trial." *BMC Fam Pract*, 12, 131.

26 S. Taki, S. Lymer, C.G. Russell et al. (2017), "Assessing user engagement of an mHealth intervention: Development and implementation of the growing healthy app engagement index." *JMIR Mhealth Uhealth*, 5, e89.

27 Neal Kaufman and Irina Khurana (2016), "Using digital health technology to prevent and treat diabetes." *Diabetes Technology & Therapeutics*, 18, Supplement 1. doi:10.1089/dia.2016.2506. https://www.ncbi.nlm.nih.gov/pmc/articles/PMC4761854/pdf/dia.2016.2506.pdf.

Opinion leader influencer mapping and management

7

The number of factors influencing physician prescribing decisions and his/her communication with patients continues to grow, including clinical experience, journal articles, CME activity, managed care, detailing, events, journal advertising, patient requests, online information seeking, etc. However, one of the most impactful influences on physicians has remained consistent: national, regional and/or local key opinion leaders (KOL). In this chapter we will explore how to accurately identify online/offline key opinion leaders to successfully promote digital health tools, initiatives, and projects aiming at empowering patients.

At the base of the importance of opinion leaders mapping and management is the critical role played by the network effect and the diffusion theory.

The *network effect* is the positive effect that an additional user of a good or service has on the value of that product to others. When a network effect is present, the value of a product or service increases according to the number of others using it.[1]

Consider for example the telephone: the higher the number of users, the higher the value to each. A positive externality, the cost or benefit that affects a party who did not choose to incur that cost or benefit, is created when a telephone is purchased without its owner intending to create value for other users, but does so regardless. Online social networks work similarly, with sites like Twitter and Facebook increasing in value to each member as more users join.

The network effect can create a bandwagon effect as the network becomes more valuable and more people join, resulting in a positive feedback loop.

Network effects become significant after a certain subscription percentage has been achieved, called critical mass. At the critical mass point, the value obtained from the good or service is greater than or equal to the price paid for the good or service. As the value of the good is determined by the user base, this implies that after a certain number of people have subscribed to the service or purchased the good, additional people will subscribe to the service or purchase the good due to the value exceeding the price.

A key business concern must then be how to attract users prior to reaching critical mass. One way is to rely on extrinsic motivation, such as a payment, a fee waiver, or a request for friends to sign up. A more natural strategy is to build a system that has enough value *without* network effects, at least to early adopters, typically customers who, in addition to using the vendor's product or technology, will also provide considerable and candid feedback to help the vendor refine its future product releases, as well as the associated means of distribution, service and support. Then, as the number of users increases, the system becomes even more valuable and is able to attract a wider user base.

Diffusion of innovations is a theory that seeks to explain how, why, and at what rate new ideas and technology spread within a social system (Rogers, 2003)[2] (see Chapter 6).

The most striking feature of diffusion theory is that, for most members of a social system, the innovation-decision depends heavily on the innovation-decisions of the other members of the system. In fact, empirically we see the successful spread of an innovation follows an S-shaped curve. After about 10–25% of system members adopt an innovation, there is relatively rapid adoption by the remaining members and then a period in which the rest of the members finally adopt. Let's review Rogers's assessment of the factors affecting the adoption of an innovation in order to see how the earlier adopters of an innovation profoundly affect the innovation-decisions of later adopters.

The innovation-decision is made through a cost-benefit analysis where the major obstacle is uncertainty. People will adopt an innovation if they believe that it will, all things considered, enhance their utility. So they must believe that the innovation may yield some relative advantage to the idea it supersedes. How can they know for sure that there are benefits? Also, in consideration of costs, people determine to what degree the innovation would disrupt other functioning facets of their daily life. Is it compatible with existing habits and values? Is it hard to use? The newness and unfamiliarity of an innovation infuse the cost-benefit analysis with a large dose of uncertainty. It sounds good, but does it work? Will it break? If I adopt it, will people think I'm weird?

Since people are on average risk-averse, the uncertainty will often result in a postponement of the decision until further evidence can be gathered. But the key is that this is not the case for everyone. Each individual's innovation-decision is largely framed by personal characteristics, and this diversity is what makes diffusion possible. For a successful innovation, the adopter distributions follow a bell-shaped curve, the derivative of the S-shaped diffusion curve, over time and approach normality (Figure 6.5).

As anticipated in Chapter 6, Rogers identifies the following main categories of consumers:

1. *Innovators (risk takers)*—are the first individuals to adopt an innovation. They are willing to take risks.
2. *Early adopters (hedgers)*—are the second fastest category to adopt an innovation.
3. *Early majority (waiters)*—the third group tends to take more time to consider adopting new innovations and is inclined to draw from feedback from early adopters before taking the risk of purchasing new products/systems.
4. *Late majority (skeptics)*—adopts the innovation after it has been established in the marketplace and is seldom willing to take risks with new innovation.
5. *Laggards (slow pokes)*—are the last to adopt an innovation. They tend to prefer traditions and are unwilling to take risks.

The personal characteristics and interaction of these groups illuminate the above-mentioned domino effect. Innovators are daring types that enjoy being on the forefront. Excited by the innovation's possible benefits they envision the opportunities and are keen to try. As early adopters use the data provided by the innovators' *implementation* and *confirmation* of the innovation to make their own adoption decisions, these two stages of the innovators' innovation-decisions are of particular value to the later decisions of potential adopters.

If opinion leaders observe that the innovation has been effective for the innovators, then they will be encouraged to adopt. This group earns respect for its judicious, well-informed decision-making, consequently it is where most opinion leaders in a social system belong. As much of the social system does not have the tendency or ability to remain up-to-date about the most recent facts about innovations, they trust the decisions made by opinion leaders. In addition, much of the social system simply wants to keep up with the rest. Since opinion leader adoption is a good indicator that an innovation is going to be adopted by many others, these conformity-loving members are encouraged to adopt. This is the famous *tipping point*, where the rate of adoption rapidly increases. The domino effect continues as, even for those who are cautious or have particular qualms with the innovation, adoption becomes a necessity as the implementation of the innovation-decisions of earlier adopters result in social and/or economic benefit (network effect). Those who have not adopted lose status or economic viability, and this contextual pressure motivates adoption.

Thus, the *tipping point* is led by opinion leader adoption. Well-informed opinion leaders communicate their approval or disapproval of an innovation, based on the innovators' experiences, to the rest of the social system. The majority respond by rapidly adopting. This analysis suggests that the spread of an innovation relies on whether or not opinion leaders endorse it.

A powerful way for *change agents* to influence the diffusion of an innovation is to shape opinion leaders' attitudes. Rogers explains that the types of opinion leaders that change agents should target depend on the nature of the social system. Social systems can be characterized as *heterophilous* or *homophilous*.

For heterophilous systems, which tend to encourage change from system norms, change agents can focus on targeting the most influential and innovative opinion leaders and the innovation will trickle down to non-influentials. If an influential opinion leader is convinced to adopt an innovation, the rest will exhibit excitement and readiness to learn and adopt it. The domino effect will commence with enthusiasm rather than resistance.

For homophilous systems, which tend toward system norms, change agents must target a wider group of opinion leaders, including some of the less influential, because innovations are less likely to trickle down. Opinion leaders who adopt innovations in homophilous systems are more likely to be regarded as suspicious and/or dismissed from their opinion leadership. Often, opinion leaders in homophilous systems avoid adopting innovations in hopes of protecting their opinion leadership. Generally, in homophilous systems, opinion leaders do not control attitudes as much as pre-existing norms do. Change agents must, if possible, communicate to opinion leaders a convincing argument in favor of the innovation that accentuates the compatibility of the innovation with system norms. The opinion leaders will then be able to use this argument, which will hopefully resonate with the masses, to support their own adoption decision.

Successful efforts to diffuse an innovation depend on characteristics of the situation. To eliminate a deficit of awareness of an innovation, mass media channels are most appropriate. To change prevailing attitudes about an innovation, it is best to persuade opinion leaders by having them use and try the new digital tool, for example.

So adoption moves like dominoes from early adopters to the early majority to the late majority to the laggards. Although thresholds operate at an individual level and vary by adopter type, at a system level, their aggregate effect is to create a critical mass that leads to a tipping point.

In the case of culturally novel and complex innovations, critical mass is seldom reached without the participation of opinion leaders. Thus, it is important to understand their characteristics and attributes.

Opinion leaders

Opinion leaders are rarely innovators and are not necessarily early adopters. Their relative position among the five adopter types depends upon the norms of the social system. Within the tradition-bound healthcare industry, the opinion leaders may be members of the early majority, refusing to adopt change without a very high standard of proof.

Roger defines opinion leadership as "the degree to which an individual is able to informally influence other individuals' attitudes or overt behavior in a desired way with relative frequency."

A key feature of opinion leaders—and one that usually makes innovators inadequate for the role—is their strong conformity to social system norms. Respect for norms is necessary to obtain the trust and commitment of other adopter types. It is important to notice that the value at play here may be less about innovation and more about power and influence. Rogers writes:

> The interpersonal relationships between opinion leaders and followers hang in a delicate balance. If an opinion leader becomes too innovative, or adopts a new idea too quickly, followers may begin to doubt his or her judgment. One role of the opinion leader in the social system is to help reduce uncertainty about an innovation. To fulfill this role, an opinion leader must demonstrate prudent judgment decisions about adopting new ideas. So the opinion leader must continually look over his or her shoulder and consider where the rest of the system is regarding new ideas.

Traditionally, opinion leaders tend to be differentiated by a number of characteristics. They tend to have/be:

1. greater connections to the outside world;
2. greater exposure to diverse media;
3. higher levels of social engagement;
4. higher socioeconomic status;
5. more innovative than followers;
6. greater exposure to change agents.

In order to measure opinion leadership and network links the following main techniques should be used:

- *Sociometric technique:* consist of asking respondents whom they sought (or hypothetically might seek) for information or advice about a given topic, such as a particular innovation. It is a highly valid measure of opinion leadership, as its information ratings are measured through the perceptions of followers. It necessitates, however, interrogating a large number of respondents in order to locate a small number of opinion leaders.
- *Self-designating technique:* asks respondents to indicate the degree to which others in the system regard them as influential. "Individuals select themselves to be peer leaders." This method depends upon the accuracy with which respondents can identify and report their images. This measure of opinion leadership is especially appropriate when interrogating a random sample of respondents in a system, a sampling design that precludes effective use of sociometric methods.
- *Observation:* an investigator identifies and records the communication behavior in a system. Opinion leaders in a system generally find a high degree of stability over time. Over a period of decades the opinion leaders in a system must inevitably change, even in a relatively stable community or organization.

Traditional vs digital key opinion leaders

With the increasing use of social media a new category of KOLs is becoming more and more important in the healthcare space: the digital KOL. As opposed to traditional KOLs, who often share thought leadership by publishing research or speaking at conferences, Digital Opinion Leaders (DOLs) use social media channels to share information and collaborate with peers. Their influence flows from their reach within a community (how many followers they have), their resonance (how much their content is shared) and their relevance (how relevant their content is to a particular objective). In recent years, DOLs with professional backgrounds have converged around Twitter as a medium for publicity and public discourse, particularly around major medical conferences, while simultaneously turning to closed healthcare provider (HCP) platforms for peer-to-peer discussions. While traditional KOLs may not have the same reach as DOLs through social media, the definitions are overlapping in some ways. Traditional KOLs are open to new tools and often engage in online speaker events to continue the conversation, while DOLs may get invited to speak at events because of their online influence. Some physician KOLs become DOLs over the years, and others may even start out as both.

DOL identification efforts tend to be fragmented and often fail to yield a repeatable process that can generate rich and actionable profiles. DOL engagement is often constrained to one-off projects, such as blogger summits, versus a sustained, continuous process of relationship building. The lack of clear organizational roles and guidelines within healthcare organizations also limits potential impact. This is pity because the emergence of the DOL is a force multiplier for healthcare peer-influence programs. A traditional KOL may have influence in terms of the articles written or the conferences at which they speak, but only a DOL has the outsize reach made possible through social media. Currently, DOLs and KOLs exist in largely different universes with little overlap. Typically, fewer than 20% of KOLs will also have a social media presence and just a handful will rank alongside DOLs in terms of online reach. By properly involving DOLs in the creation of programs and by regularly sharing with them, life sciences communicators have a built-in megaphone that can expand the authenticity and reach of their messages, as DOLs willingly amplify messages across their social networks. Engaging with DOLs involves mapping online communities of interest, identifying and profiling DOLs within those communities, and then engaging with them.

Identifying digital opinion leaders

DOLs provide thought leadership to peer physicians but also to patients and the general public. People interested in health and well-being often follow healthcare professionals on social media to receive trusted advice.

You may have to do some general searching in the specific therapeutic area before you know which physician profiles to analyze. Start by searching for the most popular and trending hashtags and monitor online conversations. Social analytic tools such as Sysomos can help identify hashtags and quickly provide an overview of influence and popularity levels. Filter out individuals from companies, and don't forget to look at physician-only networks, such as Doximity and Sermo, in addition to common social media channels.

To identify thought leaders in the digital space, you will need to look at both quantitative and qualitative aspects:

- Quantitative: reach (amount of followers/fans), frequency of postings, resonance (mentions, shares).
- Qualitative: Relevance of content and audience. Specifically, ask yourself: What are common topics and disease states? What brands/products are mentioned? Does the content speak to physicians, patients, or the general public?

The qualitative aspect may require some additional research on the physician's online activity on external sites. Once you have a list going of identified DOLs, consider looking at what sources and physicians they collectively follow.

Current top followed physicians include Dr. Kevin Pho, also known as KevinMD (@KevinMD), and Dr. Sanjay Gupta (@DrSanjayGupta). Both of them have a large following on Twitter, and KevinMD also has a well-known blog.

Identifying traditional KOLs

As they are well known in their local community but may appear in fewer and less optimized search results, traditional KOLs might be more challenging to identify. They typically have a voice in their community, publish research, and frequently speak at conferences and events.

To identify traditional KOLs, the following sources can be a good starting point:

- Top rated physicians by their peers and/or patients (i.e. patients associations).
- Advisory board volunteers of professional member organizations, or specific organizations for a given specialty.
- Authors of published research in professional journals.
- Speakers at national conferences and local events.

Change agents

A change agent is defined as "an individual who influences clients' innovation-decisions in a direction deemed desirable by the change agency" (Rogers, 2003).[3] Their biggest impact is felt during the weak early stage of diffusion.

In dealing with complex or novel innovations, change agents are necessary to fill gaps in technical knowledge and know-how. In these cases change agents typically have a considerably greater technical competence than members of the "client" social system. Unfortunately, this superior know-how often creates communication and cultural gaps that are difficult to bridge.

When the desired change is complex and affects social and cultural norms, the change agent's job is enormously difficult. Rogers observes:

> As a bridge between two differing systems, the change agent is a marginal figure with one foot in each of two worlds. In addition to facing this problem with social marginality, change agents also must deal with the problem of *information overload*, the state of an individual or a system in

which excessive communication inputs cannot be processed and utilized, leading to breakdown. By understanding the needs of the clients, the change agent can selectively transmit to them only information that is relevant.

Main Change Agent Roles include:

- Developing need for change.
- Establishing an information-exchange relationship.
- Diagnosing their problems.
- Creating intent to change in the client.
- Translating intent into action.
- Stabilizing adoption and preventing discontinuances.
- Achieving a terminal relationship.

As a consequence, efforts of change agents include:

1. *Making contact with clients:* Frequent contact builds familiarity and creates opportunities to establish credibility and trust.
2. *Client orientation:* Is the change agent trying to solve the clients' problem or trying to advance their own agenda (e.g., make a sale)? If the change agent is listening, they can learn ways to modify and improve their innovation.
3. *Client empathy:* A change agent is more effective when he/she can see the world through the eyes of the client.
4. *Homophily with clients:* Can the change agent look and act like an insider? In the legal industry, change agents with law degrees generally have an easier time because of a common experience and background with most clients.
5. *Credibility in the clients' eyes:* Can the change agent fluidly answer tough questions? If the client must trust the change agents' judgment, do the change agents possess the credentials and background to understand the underlying innovation?
6. *Working thru Opinion Leaders:* Rogers observes, "The time and energy of the change agents are scarce resources" (p. 388). Engaging opinion leaders is the most efficient path to system wide success.
7. *Improving technical competence of clients:* Clients dislike long-term dependency on change agents. Thus, effective change agents often make education the cornerstone of their efforts, which builds trust and enables clients to make future adoption decisions on their own.

Key opinion leaders mapping

Identifying and engaging the right key scientific leaders can be a challenging task. With today's capabilities to capture technology-driven data, KOL mapping is of peculiar importance at this aim.

KOL mapping is a quantitative approach used to evaluate forward-thinking leadership by applying specific filters and analytics to data-driven activities and peer networks. Mapping allows you to pinpoint leadership by measuring the visibility and influence of physicians around the world.

New methodologies of identifying scientific leaders are far-reaching: they look for innovation in research, academic, and publication status, collaborations, behaviors in the treatment of patients, and experience in seeing a product or digital tool achieve market access. In addition, mapping considers both local networks and international networks. An innovative medical communications agency might offer many strategies that can help guide organizations in identifying and engaging with the most influential thought leaders in their field.

KOL mapping provides insight into the reputation, importance or leadership of targeted experts. Approaches to mapping someone's professional status include bibliometric, patient diagnosis and referral, and sociometric data analysis. Mapping strategies depend on a company's needs, but often look at the leaders' peer networks. Ultimately, scientific leaders can be evaluated not only for their achievements, but also for their specific contributions in research or with regard to a defined therapeutic field.

Database-driven KOL mapping can be tailored to match an organization' objective; the various assets of a KOL are given a value and isolated to form an independent network. At this stage, various filters and measures can be applied to the network to determine the best match for a partnership. Relationships, or links, can be assessed to comprehend a thought leader's professional status. Factors that help describe leadership or reputation are measured, such as the frequency of interactions and connectivity. Determining the right data sources with appropriate influence and network analytics is critical to get the best results from KOL mapping.

The ability to use data to understand and identify expertise is extremely important for companies seeking a partnership. For example, KOL mapping has the potential to provide insight into the care pathway for a relevant therapy, or new digital tool which in turn can inform future trial and/or digital tool design. This typically occurs at a local level. So finding someone in a peer leadership role who considers how a treatment or a digital tool is adopted by local communities and caregivers may be as valuable to a company, if not more, as influence demonstrated on a global or national level.

Moreover, technology increasingly supports the transparency of regulatory changes and therefore invites scrutiny from physicians, which are commonly mentioned through peer networks. In fact, technology today allows exploring deeper into KOL behaviors and opinions than ever before. So when companies are looking to be matched with forward-thinking leaders, KOL mapping, done correctly, can help identify physicians or experts who've created buzz surrounding a certain topic. This is especially relevant when planning the introduction process or considering a product/service's branding position.

How to accurately identify digital key opinion leaders

When identifying KOLs, the quality of candidates will be reflected in how well they help you achieve your objective.

As a matter of fact, selecting the right KOLs isn't just about effort, it is also, and most importantly, about applying a careful and objective approach to the first step on the journey: candidate identification and profiling.[4]

To ensure your initial candidate list is "fit for purpose" it is wise to adopt a systematic approach to the identification, profiling and mapping of candidates. This not only finds the best candidates for your needs but also allows you to re-run your selection process at a later time using different qualification thresholds letting you review how the landscape may have changed.

A systematic approach should include the following five steps.

Step 1: Define your variables: Landscape, objectives, profile and scale

Landscape: What is the therapeutic field in which you work? Can it be broken down into different specialties? Focus on expertise: What 'additional' expertise do you need be represented within your KOL team to facilitate delivery of your objectives: experience of competitor landscape, unmet needs, level of pharmacologic knowledge, level of digital knowledge, level of experience with digital tools within your therapeutic area, including your digital tools, population modeling, health economists and/or patient advocates? Also, make sure to build for the future early in the process. What kind of changes you oversee ahead and at will their impact be on your requirements?

Objective: What do you need your KOLs to achieve in supporting your future projects? Define what you would like in the form of S.M.A.R.T. derived objectives. KOLs are often involved in professional education, clinical research advisory boards and delivering strategic communications as well as serving on medical policy and guideline boards. Will these help promote your activities?

The planned landscape and activities in which KOLs are involved will define the profile of the ideal candidate. Thus, you will need to identify opportunities for KOLs to engage and support activities that will bring your objectives to life.

Scope: How many KOLs do you need to implement your plans and achieve your objectives? What geographical area are you planning to cover: global, national or local? Will your requirements change with time? Plan for the full lifecycle of your project or program. To prevent any unforeseen delay, plan to identify around twice to three times the number of KOLs you estimate you will need. Is the therapy area well supplied with candidates?

The pool of researchers will be smaller for rarer diseases and disorders, and therefore fewer candidates are likely to be available than better served therapy areas—it may also mean that fewer will be required to influence opinion within the field.

Profile: Knowing the landscape and objectives will give you an insight into the key attributes your ideal KOL will embody. A list of possible characteristics you may want to consider and/or avoid when identifying potential candidates is provided below. How you prioritize each of these attributes will depend on your specific challenge:

- Investigators of clinical trials and authors of journal articles and treatment guidelines
- High therapy area profile
- Editorial board members of journals and officers of professional associations
- Positions of responsibility in hospital and university departments
- Speakers at conventions and symposia
- Excellent communication skills, accomplished networker with charisma: the 'X' factor!

Step 2: Search and score

The outputs derived from Step 1 will inform your decisions on what characteristics will best describe the type of KOL you want and guide your search. In this age of sophisticated Internet search engines and transparency in professional interests there is a wealth of information about potential candidates available. Though the Internet simplifies the process of data collection, you might need to plan an extensive amount of time for this stage as you might need to visit multiple information sources to obtain a thorough set of data. As you are not just collecting a list of names, make sure to set a target with a definable endpoint and/or delivery time line at which searching will stop and you review your progress, before you start searching for information. This, besides saving you time later by providing a clear delivery pathway and minimizing duplication of searches, it will also make the process reproducible (if you want to retrace your steps at a later date) and open to scrutiny as to whether or not you have taken an objective approach.

In developing a search strategy, develop a list of the sources you will search for data on the key characteristics you are hoping to capture. For example:

Sources: Identify potential sources you plan to search for the required information. Where possible list the search terms you expect to use. Data sources may include:

- Patient associations
- Publication databases
- Journals that cover the therapy area
- Scientific societies
- Congress meetings
- University and hospital websites

Characteristics

- Activity in delivering medicine
- Involvement in defining medical practice and teaching
- Involvement in research

Step 3: Analyze, rank and identify

Having collected all the needed information and data, you now need to analyze them in order to rank candidates. The key to successful ranking is to develop an algorithm that will identify the candidates most closely reflecting the predefined perfect candidate. The most straightforward approach to ranking is called the *Objective Ranking System* which utilizes specific variables that you should score according to your predefined scale. The process is completely objective and provides an unbiased account of the professional landscape for a given set of parameters. An alternative approach, *Peer Qualification* provides an excellent approach to ranking. A panel of peers is asked to score each expert against predefined criteria. The results are summed to produce a final ranking.

At the end of the ranking process, you will have an ordered list of the right number of qualifying thought leaders. To complete the identification process simply select your top scoring candidates. You may want to further interrogate your list before selecting candidates—for example, if you want to select individuals that can represent specific geographical territories—this can be achieved easily enough if you have collected the relevant information from the outset. You are not limited to one analysis. Change the weighting to see how it affects the score of your candidates. You may want to identify your good presenters, good investigators and/or those good at publishing in scientific literature.

Step 4: Profile

Once the required number of thought leaders has been identified you need to build more specific profiles of the KOL candidates that will give you a greater insight into how they are going to fit together as a team.

Outline their career background, research areas, track record and other interests. This should empower you to be able to get a clearer picture of your candidates to understand better who would be the best individuals to recruit as thought leaders. Use all the facilities you have at your disposal—university websites are usually a good starting point.

> "To change prevailing attitudes about an innovation, it is best to persuade opinion leaders by having them use and try the new digital tool."

Notes

1 Carl Shapiro and Hal R. Varian (1999), *Information Rules*. Brighton, MA: Harvard Business School Press.
2 E.M. Rogers (2003), *Diffusion of Innovations*, 5th edition. New York: Free Press.
3 E.M. Rogers (2003), *Diffusion of Innovations*, 5th edition. New York: Free Press.
4 Justin Cook (2016), *Looking Out for a Hero! An Insider's Insight into Key Opinion Leader Identification and Profiling*. Niche Science & Technology Ltd, UK. [online]. Available at http://www.niche.org.uk/asset/insider-insight/Insider-KOLIP-P.pdf [Accessed March 23, 2018].

Part III

Actions and tools to help physicians empower their patients

Patient empowerment 8

A process and
an outcome

Empowerment-based interventions include both a process and an outcome component. The process component occurs when the true purpose of the intervention is to increase the patient's capacity to think critically and make autonomous, informed decisions. The outcome component occurs when there is a measurable increase in the patient's ability to make autonomous, informed decisions. In this chapter we are going to explore both traditional and digital methods and tools physicians can use to inform, engage, involve and empower patients.

We'll begin our journey with a **leading case history** on patient engagement in action at the Multiple Sclerosis in the21st Century initiative which is led by a Steering Group of international experts in MS treatment and management, and by patient group representatives.[1] The initiative seeks to define MS treatment and standards of care for the twenty-first century, develop a minimum standard of care internationally, and motivate the MS community to align standards of care and challenge the current treatment paradigm. Understanding of patient engagement in MS is in its infancy but the factors influencing engagement appear complex and diverse. One cross-sectional survey of 199

MS patients in Southeast USA, identified that MS-related QoL and MS-related self-efficacy correlated significantly with patient activation in MS patients (r=0.42, Po0.01 and r=0.50, Po0.01, respectively). Depression had an inverse correlation (r=0.43; Po0.01) (Goodworth et al, 2014).[2] Studies in other disease areas have demonstrated further elements that may play a role. One review reported five categories of factors influencing engagement: patient-related (patients' knowledge/beliefs, demographic characteristics, emotions and coping style); illness-related (symptoms, treatment plan, patient's prior experience, illness severity); healthcare professional (HCP)-related (HCPs' knowledge and beliefs, HCP role); healthcare setting-related (primary or secondary care);and task-related (medical knowledge required and whether the required patient behavior challenges clinicians' clinical abilities) (Davis et al., 2007).[3]

Understanding the issues that influence patient engagement in MS will facilitate investigation into how these might be overcome.

Setting and facilitating engagement by education and confidence-building in MS

A prerequisite to helping a patient become engaged is the establishment of an effective, caring and mutually respectful patient–physician relationship; patients consistently say that good communication with their doctors boosts their confidence with the healthcare process (von Puckler, 2013;[4] Duffy et al., 2004).[5] People prefer to be treated by clinicians who are empathetic listeners and who are good at informing, advising and educating them (Coulter, 2005;[6] Keating et al., 2002).[7] Moreover, the main independent predictors of patient satisfaction are patients' perceptions of communication and partnership, and a positive approach by the doctor (Little et al., 2001).[8]

Engagement is vital from the day of diagnosis (Solari, 2014) when the MS patient and their physician embark on a unique journey together and the emotional burden on both parties is high (Solari, 2014).[9] Consequently, the collaborative nature of that initial process and the success in instigating clear, honest communication can determine whether the future relationship will be one of trust and respect and how positively the patient will be involved in their health decisions and management.

Various practical strategies have been proposed to optimize physician–patient communication. Simple *conversational and listening techniques* can be helpful, such as sitting down during a consultation, attending to patient comfort, establishing eye contact, listening without interrupting, showing attention with nonverbal cues such as nodding, allowing silences while patients search for words, acknowledging and legitimizing feelings, explaining and reassuring during examinations, and asking explicitly if there are other areas of concern.

The provision of *'prompt sheets'* encourages patients to ask questions about their treatment options, patients can be encouraged to bring a list of questions to their clinic visits. Directing patients to access their medical notes promotes transparency and trust, and improves information recall. Tools such as www.myopennotes.org provide help in achieving this. However, patients with low levels of health literacy may find this initially challenging. A 'road map' or a set of goals that both physician and patient wish to achieve can be developed and amended throughout the disease course.

Shea (2006)[10] also describes a number of useful techniques, such as: learning the patient's belief set; familiarization with the patient's family history/cultural beliefs to discover underlying motivations; providing the patient with a sense of collaboration in the health decision process; and learning the patient's opinion toward taking medication in general. In addition, reliable, up-to-date publications and guidance to support physicians in communicating with their patients are provided by the MS Society.

The Adopt One! Challenge,[11] for example, allows physicians to obtain a comprehensive baseline assessment of their patient communication skills, measure how their skills compare with best practice, and access online skills development tools. The program encourages physicians to commit to adopting one new patient-centered communication skill over the course of 12 months and provides online training and resources needed to help them achieve this goal.

Current management guidelines underline the importance of educating and supporting the MS patient. National Institute for Clinical Excellence (NICE) guidelines recommend implementing an education program that takes into account the different aspects of the disease and incorporates guidance on the level of communication, provision of emotional support, encouragement of autonomy/self-management and provision of support to family and carers; the European MS Platform's Code of Good Practice stresses the importance of accessible information, informed advice and emotional support, and suggests self-help education programs be provided for patients and their carers. The concept of 'therapeutic patient education' has also been enshrined in French law (article 84, Hospitals, Patients, Health and Territory, LawNo.2009–879of 21July2009) and is officially recognized as an integral part of patient care. Specifically, it mandates that patients must receive specialized education related to their condition, which can be delivered by trained "peer educators."

Successful physicians have one thing in common: they share and commit to the values and methods presented by the Multiple Sclerosis in the21st Century Initiative. They are extremely patient-centered and greatly committed to making patient empowerment happen.

Successful patient empowerment relies not just on new technology but also on a cultural shift.

There are many ways to get the ball rolling to change the way physicians interact with their patients and to get them to play an active role in their care, to begin, here are a few ideas:

1. *Encourage patients to update and share their medication details:* Being able to share their medication history—including an account of medications being taken, previous prescription details and any contra-indications, would be helpful for physicians while also helping patients stay conscientious about their prescriptions.
2. *Encourage patients to update their allergies and previous health concerns:* Patients may not always remember to provide physicians with a complete picture of their health, including information about all their allergies and previous health concerns. Encouraging them to update these details would help physicians make informed decisions about their care and prevent health complications.
3. *Tell patients about sharing information from their wearable devices:* Physicians can't keep a watch on your patients all day. But they already have a smart-watch or activity tracker doing that every day. Apps like ContinuousCare,[12] for example, allow patients to sync data from their wearable devices so that they can then share these vital parameters with their physicians. Most home health monitoring devices, like iHealth devices, also allow users to view and track their measured vitals on their mobile, allowing them to stay on track with their health goals.
4. *Promote remote care to get patients to take control of their health:* One of the other ways to empower patients would be to promote self-management of chronic diseases. It has been hypothesized that self-reporting of health parameters, self-care interventions and the use of healthcare services can be improved significantly by empowering patients. Services such as the Virtual Practice's Remote Monitoring allow health providers to engage and empower their patients by defining home care plans for patients with chronic illnesses. Patients update their health parameters periodically for review by their care providers, thereby managing their health at home and reducing the risk of unhealthy inconsistencies in their condition. In addition to getting providers and patients to actively communicate with one another between hospital visits, remote monitoring can also prevent health complications through continuous care and review—a benefit for those with chronic illnesses.
5. *Allow your patients to consult with you online:* Permitting patients to ask questions online provides them with the right information about their health, as opposed to relying on information from online sources. This empowers

them to take the right decisions for their care and adhere to medical advice from their physicians. The growth of online consultation services like HealthTap has allowed patients to get answers to their health queries without having to wait for their next appointment, providing quicker and easier access to healthcare services.

6. *Encourage patients to connect through video consultations:* Telemedicine has indeed been a benefit in terms of increasing the accessibility of healthcare. For one, it has allowed patients to consult with their health providers irrespective of geographical location. Setting up a telemedicine service helps patients with chronic illnesses, senior citizens, and patients who may not be able to make it to their appointments. Providing these patients with an alternative means of connecting with their providers improves their health outcomes while ensuring patient satisfaction. Unlike Skype, video consultations allow doctors and patients to securely share and edit health records.

7. *Educate to empower your patients:* Patient education can go a long way in helping patients understand important aspects of their health and care. Reappraising myths, demystifying complex procedures and treatments and describing health-related concerns will allow patients to get a better understanding on options for their healthcare. Platforms like the Health Network and WebMD aim at creating a health community involving both physicians and patients to discuss relevant topics about health and well-being. Instead of relying on unverified external sources, patients on the Health Network can be confident that the information and health tips available to them on the network are reliable. With specific mobile apps for doctors and patients, the Health Network can be accessed on a smartphone, making it even easier to educate and empower patients. Health providers being involved in educating their patients also have the additional advantage of limiting self-diagnosis and treatment, which can have devastating consequences on patient well-being.

8. *Allow patients to schedule appointments online:* Online appointment scheduling, such as the one offered by the Virtual Practice™ and similar online appointment scheduling solutions allow patients to be more proactive in their care. Instead of waiting to connect with the doctor's office by telephone, patients now have the option to book an appointment at a time convenient to them, at any time of the day. Automated reminders also ensure that the chances of no-shows are greatly reduced, helping providers to make the most of their day. Tools such as the Virtual Practice™ from ContinuousCare offers health providers and healthcare organizations the necessary tools to facilitate patient empowerment through patient

engagement services like video consultation, telehealth services, remote care and practice management services like appointment scheduling and revenue management. Learn more.

Empowerment-based interventions include both a process and an outcome component

Paulo Freire viewed empowerment as both a process and an outcome. Empowerment is a process when the purpose of an educational intervention is to increase one's ability to think critically and act autonomously. Empowerment is an outcome when an enhanced sense of self-efficacy occurs as a result of the process. However, while empowerment is an outcome, it is not a dichotomous variable, in that one is or is not empowered. Instead, empowerment is a continuous variable, more similar to a direction than a location. As an example, when using the Diabetes Empowerment Scale (DES), the strength and direction of change is an indication of the intervention's effectiveness.[13]

As an analogy, if the goal of compliance-based education is to go east, then the goal of empowerment-based education is to go west. The question becomes, how far west must one go to be considered western? Robert M. Anderson et al.'s (2010) answer is as far west as one is willing and able to go. Thus, the process and outcome are different for each of us.

Empowerment-based interventions include both a process and an outcome component. The process component occurs when the true purpose of the intervention is to increase the patient's capacity to think critically and make autonomous, informed decisions. The outcome component occurs when there is a measurable increase in the patient's ability to make autonomous, informed decisions.

In their study exploring the empowerment of diabetes patients, Anderson et al. state that the foundational principles of empowerment are based on observation and logical reasoning. HCPs are responsible for doing all that they can to ensure their patients are equipped to make decisions informed by an adequate understanding of diabetes self-management and an awareness of the aspects of their personal lives that influence their self-management decisions.

The socialization of HCPs to take responsibility for their patients' care and outcomes conflicts with the existential fact that patients control and are responsible for 98% of that care. HCPs often exercise their perceived responsibility by telling patients how to manage their diabetes on a daily basis even though they lack the control to ensure that their recommendations are carried out. For many patients these recommended behavior changes are difficult and in some cases impossible to carry out. HCPs often experience frustration at their unsuccessful attempts at persuasion and they blame their patients for failing to achieve recommended outcomes, labeling them as noncompliant. Many patients also become frustrated because they are unable to carry out their HCPs recommendations and often feel blamed by their HCPs.

Anderson et al. (2010) articulated a five-step approach to setting behavioral goals (Table 8.1) which provides patients with the information and clarity they need to develop and reach their diabetes- and lifestyle-related goals. The first two steps are to define the problem and ascertain patients' beliefs, thoughts and feelings that may support or hinder their efforts. The third is to identify long-term goals toward which patients will work. Patients then choose and commit to making a behavioral change that will help them to achieve their long-term

Table 8.1 Behavior-change protocol

Step I: Explore the Problem or Issue (Past)
What is the hardest thing about caring for your diabetes?
Please tell me more about that.
Are there some specific examples you can give me?
Step II: Clarify Feelings and Meaning (Present)
What are your thoughts about this?
Are you feeling (insert feeling) because (insert meaning)?
Step III: Develop a Plan (Future)
What do you want?
How would this situation have to chance for you to feel better about it?
Where would you like to be regarding this situation in (specific time, e.g. 1 month,
    3 months, 1 year)?
What are your options?
What are barriers for you?
Who could help you?
What are the costs and benefits for each of your choices?
What would happen if you do not do anything about it?
How important is it, on a scale of 1 to 10, for you to do something about this?
Let's develop a plan.
Step IV: Commit to Action (Future)
Are you willing to do what you need to do to solve this problem?
What are some steps you could take?
What are you going to do?
When are you going to do it?
How will you know if you have succeeded?
What is one thing you will do when you leave here today?
Step V: Experience and Evaluate the Plan (Future)
How did it go?
What did you learn?
What barriers did you encounter?
What, if anything, would you do differently next time?
What will you do when you leave here today?

Source: Martha M. Funnell and Robert M. Anderson (2004), *Clin Diabetes*, 22, 123–127.

goals. The final step is for patients to evaluate their efforts and identify what they learned in the process.

Helping patients view this process as behavioral experiments eliminates the concepts of success and failure. Instead, all efforts are opportunities to learn more about the true nature of the problem, related feelings, barriers and effective strategies. The role of the provider is to provide information, collaborate during the goal-setting process, and offer support for patients' efforts.

While they used active listening skills during this process, other non-directive communication strategies, such as motivational interviewing, may also be used to the same end.

The purpose of goal-setting in the empowerment approach is to help patients become more autonomous and learn how to make self-selected behavior changes, rather than trying to convince them to comply with goals that have been established by HCPs.

Correcting common misconceptions the empowerment approach to care

In their article, Anderson et al. (2010) try to clarify the meaning of empowerment by correcting common misconceptions based on what HCPs have said to them or that they have found in the scientific literature.[14] Following is a selection of some of the most common misconceptions.

Examples of not seeing what is there

Misconception: "I want to empower my patients to improve compliance/adherence." "Empowerment means patients doing everything they should."

Empowerment is the antithesis of compliance. The purpose of empowerment-based interventions is to help patients learn to think critically and make informed decisions. There are certainly times when patients' decisions are congruent with their HCP's recommendations. After all, patients generally want to be healthy and prevent the complications of diabetes. There also will be times when patients make informed decisions that are not compatible with the recommendations made by their HCP. Healthcare providers may know what is clinically best for a patient's diabetes; however, that does not mean that HCPs know what is best for that patient's life. We have defined noncompliance simply as two people working toward different goals. Shifting away from compliance-based approaches gives us the opportunity to create collaborative partnerships with our patients where we can work toward common, patient identified goals.

Misconception: "Empowerment-based education means you only focus on the patient's issues."

Many empowerment-based education programs are "lecture-free" and content is presented based on the questions and concerns raised by the participants. The role of the HCP is to serve as a facilitator and expert resource for this process. Generally, the HCP either answers questions directly or asks participants about their experiences with the concerns raised. This approach does not mean that HCPs are absolved of their educational responsibilities, nor does it mean patients are left to find critical information on their own. It is up to the HCP to ensure that patients have the knowledge and resources to make thoughtful decisions. Once the patients' questions and concerns have been addressed, the HCP discusses other issues that need to be addressed (i.e. taking insulin safely, treatment of hypoglycemia). HCPs are also responsible for raising their own concerns and helping patients understand the consequences of their decisions, while acknowledging the reality that the final choice is in the hands of the patient.

Examples of seeing what is not there

Misconception: "… responsibility for these patients' health outcomes lies fully and wholly with the patients themselves."

This is not an assumption that we make. Health outcomes are dependent on many factors including genetics, self-management decisions, the quality and quantity of healthcare patients receive, and financial and other resources, to name a few. However, we do assert that patients are responsible for the consequences of their diabetes self-management decisions. These consequences are but one factor (albeit an important one) among many factors that account for patients' health outcomes.

Misconception: Empowerment assumes "… the HCP simply helps patients to acquire the knowledge and skills necessary to make well informed choices about diabetes self-management."

This statement is incorrect on two fronts. First, we have asserted that the role of the HCP using the empowerment approach goes well beyond "simply helps patients to acquire the knowledge and skills." We believe that HCPs are responsible for helping patients achieve their goals and overcome barriers through education, appropriate care recommendations, expert advice, self-reflection, and social and self-management support. Secondly, regarding support, our view of empowerment has always included the need for ongoing psychosocial and diabetes self-management support (DSMS) following initial diabetes education.

Whether the misconception statements above are based on HCPs beliefs or on assumptions HCPs believe Anderson et al. (2010) have made, they all stem from a fundamental misunderstanding of the empowerment approach to diabetes care and education. The empowerment approach does NOT involve convincing, persuading, "empowering" or changing patients (or getting them to change). Empowerment does not involve doing something to patients.

The empowerment approach involves facilitating and supporting patients to reflect on their experience of living with diabetes. Self-reflection occurring in a relationship characterized by psychological safety, warmth, collaboration and respect is essential for laying the foundation for self-directed positive change in behavior, emotions and/or attitudes. Such reflection often leads to their enhanced awareness and understanding of the consequences of their self-management decisions.

Traditional methods and tools physicians can use to inform, engage, involve and empower patients

Regardless the increasing use of digital tools, traditional methods such as physician–patient communication and shared decision-making still play a critical role in making patient empowerment successful and able to create value.

Communication tools

Several useful communication techniques, such as motivational interviewing, can promote certain health behaviors and adherence to treatment regimens by drawing out the patients' motivation for change (Rollnick et al., 2008).[15] There is also a need for research on interventions that can improve a patient's ability to manage health information (Berkman et al., 2011).[16]

A number of studies show that patients, their families and other caregivers can bring useful and often critically important knowledge to bear on care if they are invited to do so. Indeed, patients often are unable to discuss all of their concerns in a single visit. Some interventions to remedy this limitation are straightforward; one study found that simply asking patients whether there was "something else" to discuss instead of "anything else" reduced the number of unmet concerns by almost 80 percent (Heritage et al., 2007).[17] Moreover, patients bring a different perspective to the encounter than clinicians and will introduce different information. For example, patients on statin drugs were far more likely than their clinician to initiate the discussion of symptoms potentially related to the prescription (Golomb et al., 2008).[18]

A variety of interventions are aimed at improving the state of patient–clinician communication (Maurer et al., 2012).[19] Opportunities to improve patient-centered communication skills exist throughout all levels of health profession education, from degree to continuing education (Levinson et al., 2010).[20] Other tools include patient coaching and question checklists, which are designed to assist patients in communicating with their clinicians. In one study, coaching and the use of checklists were shown to increase the number of questions patients asked and were associated with a modest improvement in patient health outcomes (Kinnersley et al., 2007).[21] The implementation of these tools has yielded some success in improving clinician communication behaviors, as well as patient knowledge and satisfaction, although evidence is mixed on the ultimate impact on patient health outcomes (Coulter and Ellins, 2006).[22] Communication tools need to be customized to patients' circumstances, especially their health literacy. Given the complexity of the field, even highly educated people may have difficulty finding and understanding health information and applying it to their own care or that of their loved ones (IOM, 2004).[23]

Shared decision-making

While informing patients about options is important, true patient-centered care requires a new model of decision-making in which responsibility is shared between patient and clinician.[24] Implementing this model will require a shift toward healthcare in which clinicians and patients work together to manage complex conditions, and make decisions on the basis of not only the best scientific evidence but also the patient's biological characteristics, preferences, values and life circumstances. Such a decision-making model is increasingly important for the growing number of clinical situations in which there are multiple care options, each with different benefits and potential harms. In these situations, where trade-offs will have to be considered, clinicians will need to discuss the risks and benefits of competing diagnostic and treatment options with patients and their caregivers (Collins et al., 2009).[25] In addition to enhanced communication techniques, tools for promoting shared decision-making include decision aids. Decision aids provide balanced information on diagnostic and treatment options, including risks and potential outcomes, and help patients consider what factors are most important to their decision. The goal is to help patients identify the diagnostic technology or treatment that best meets their needs, goals and circumstances. Studies of such tools have found that they increase patients' knowledge and understanding of benefits and risks and encourage them to participate in decisions (Arterburn et al., 2011;[26] Belkora et al., 2012;[27] O'Connor et al., 2004,[28] 2007a,b;[29] Solberg et al., 2010;[30] Stacey et al., 2011).[31] Several organizations, including the International Patient Decision Aids Standards Collaboration, have developed standards against which to validate the quality of decision aids and ensure that they are accurate, unbiased and understandable. The concept of patient-centered care entails customizing care according to patient preferences along all dimensions, including the level of involvement in decision-making. Some patients will be interested in playing a strong role in care decisions, while others may want to play a less active role. Evidence suggests that the system currently does not allow patients to realize their desired level of participation; in one study, fewer than half of patients reported they had achieved their preferred level of control in decision-making (Degner et al., 1997).[32] Several studies confirm that while most patients wish to be asked their opinions and be offered choices in their care, patients differ in how they would like to be involved in final care decisions (Chung et al., 2011;[33] Deber et al., 2007;[34] Fineberg, 2012;[35] Levinson et al., 2005;[36] Solberg et al., 2009).[37] These studies illustrate the complex role of patient autonomy in the provision of patient-centered care and confirm the variability in the preferences of individual patients and patient populations in this aspect of care. They also signal that patient satisfaction requires patient–clinician communication that not only shares the appropriate clinical information for each patient, but also provides the appropriate amount of information and degree of autonomy in acting on the information. These findings suggest as well that it is important for clinicians to be working in an environment where they can function as careful listeners and coaches, as well as experts in their field.

Effective patient–clinician communication and shared decision-making are key components of patient-centered care. These components require that informed, activated and participatory patients and family members interact with a patient-centered care team that has effective communication skills and is supported by an accessible, well-organized and responsive healthcare system (Epstein and Street, 2007).[38] As described by the NCI's monograph *Patient-Centered Communication in Cancer Care*, the primary functions of patient-centered communication are to (1) foster healing relationships, (2) exchange information, (3) respond to emotions, (4) manage uncertainty, (5) make decisions, and (6) enable patient self-management (Epstein and Street, 2007).[39] These six functions dynamically interact to influence the quality of patient–clinician interactions and may ultimately influence patients' health outcomes (Epstein and Street, 2007).[40] They are skills that need to be developed, utilized, and maintained across the cancer care continuum.

Challenges for clinicians

A number of factors can prevent clinicians from engaging in patient-centered communication and shared decision-making, including clinicians' lack of training in communication (see section below on prioritizing clinician training in communication) and insensitivity to patients' informational, cultural, and emotional needs. Clinician characteristics, such as age, gender, and training, may influence the provision of patient-centered communication (Epstein and Street, 2007;[41] Porter-O'Grady and Malloch, 2007).[42] For example, some older clinicians may use authoritative communication styles rather than more collaborative approaches (Busari, 2013;[43] Frosch et al., 2012).[44]

Epstein and Street (2007)[45] noted that some clinicians fail to appreciate the range of patient and family needs, explaining, in part, patients and their families' dissatisfaction with the timing and amount of information given to them by clinicians. As mentioned previously, clinicians need to be aware of the differing informational needs of patients and adapt their communication approach accordingly (Epstein and Street, 2007;[46] IOM, 2011a).[47] A clinician's level of comfort discussing specific aspects of cancer care can also impede patient-centered communication and shared decision-making. Research shows that clinicians are often uncomfortable discussing poor prognoses, psychosocial and emotional aspects of care, and sexuality (Epstein and Street, 2007;[48] IOM, 2008a;[49] Mack and Smith, 2012).[50] Furthermore, clinicians may not recognize patients' emotional cues and may be unfamiliar with resources and services designed to meet patients' psychosocial health needs (Epstein and Street, 2007;[51] IOM, 2008a).[52]

Clinicians can also misjudge patient preferences. For example, clinicians may expect women with early stage breast cancer to prefer to keep their breast, given that mastectomy and lumpectomy followed by radiation can be equally effective treatment options for some patients. A study of breast cancer patients who were provided comprehensive information about both treatment options, however, found that approximately one-third of women chose to have a mastectomy (Collins et al., 2009).[53] Other patients may prioritize quality of life rather than length of life as a primary goal (Berman, 2012;[54] IOM, 2011a).[55] In addition, patients with cancer may assess the benefits and risks of chemotherapy differently than their clinicians, and may be more willing to undergo chemotherapy with small benefits and high risks of toxicity (Matsuyama et al., 2006).[56]

Differences between patients' and clinicians' culture and language may influence clinicians' ability to engage in patient-centered communication and shared decision-making. Surbone (2010, p. 4)[57] emphasized that language and cultural barriers can be a major source of stress for patients, family members, and clinicians, especially if "linguistic, health literacy, and cultural differences combined render mutual understanding especially difficult." Clinicians' and patients' mutual misunderstanding can result in frustration and mistrust, negatively impacting the care received by patients with cancer (Surbone, 2010).[58] Epstein and Street (2007)[59] noted that cultural beliefs will affect communication between clinicians and patients, influence how patients and clinicians interpret their interaction, and impact communication outcomes. Clinicians' lack of time may also limit the provision of patient-centered communication and shared decision-making.

System-level challenges

The fragmented nature of the care system can prohibit patient-centered communication and shared decision-making (IOM and NRC, 1999).[60] Epstein and Street (2007)[61] emphasized that patient-centered communication and shared decision-making relies on more than the patient–clinician interactions; it also includes the physical and procedural characteristics of the healthcare system. Patients who find it difficult to navigate the healthcare system are likely to experience lower quality patient–clinician communication and shared decision-making, which could contribute to underutilization of high-quality care, overuse of care that is unlikely to improve patient outcomes, and higher costs.

Fragmentation of the care delivery system also contributes to communication problems between patients and their care teams. Patients with cancer, for example, may need to coordinate care among multiple clinicians on their cancer care team and other care teams. Jessie Gruman, a four-time cancer survivor, pointed out that in one year, eight physicians cared for her, and yet only once did two of those physicians communicate directly with each other; she was primarily responsible for sharing her medical information among the different clinicians (Gruman, 2013).[62] It can be especially difficult for care team members to share information and communicate effectively with patients if the care team members' electronic health records (EHRs) are not interoperable (see Chapter 7 on additional information technology challenges). With system problems such as these, it can be unclear to patients and care teams who is responsible for each aspect of care and who needs to be contacted to address a treatment complication (IOM, 2011a).[63] New models of care and reimbursement, such as accountable care organizations (ACOs) may address some of these system challenges.[64]

Engaging patients at the organizational level

Patient-centered care goes beyond direct patient–clinician interactions to the clinic, unit, and healthcare organization level.[65] At this level, patient-centeredness means different things, such as creating patient and family councils, establishing portals that allow patients to access their health information, and developing policies that ensure timely access to care (Balik et al., 2011;[66] Maurer et al., 2012).[67] Given that patients, their families and other caregivers are the people who actually experience care, their perspectives can contribute substantially to effective and efficient healthcare organizations. Leveraging their knowledge can improve the experience of care through the application of their insights to the design and delivery of care in healthcare organizations—from hospital design, to visiting hours, to care delivery (Bergeson and Dean, 2006;[68] Groene, 2011;[69] Johnson et al., 2008;[70] Scholle et al., 2010).[71] Thus involving patients in improvement initiatives ensures that patients' values and perspectives guide system design, in addition to keeping the teams working on these projects focused on patient priorities. There are several successful approaches for improving the patient experience, such as those focused on reducing waiting times (Litvak and Bisognano, 2011;[72] Litvak et al., 2005),[73] which also can improve quality and reduce costs. To further center care on patient needs and preferences, healthcare organizations and systems can act on lessons learned about what patients value by engaging patients, their families and other caregivers. For example, systems can ensure the inclusion of patient perspectives in an institution's operations by promoting patient and family participation on advisory councils, giving patients and their families direct access to the institution's decision-making structures. Case studies have shown that by working on such councils, patients may participate in institutional quality improvement projects, help redesign service delivery processes, serve on search committees for new executives, and help develop educational programs for hospital staff. They also may aid the hospital in making its procedures more efficient and patient-centered and may participate in rounds, which can lead to new suggestions for improvement (Balik et al., 2011;[74] Conway et al., 2006;[75] Ponte et al., 2003).[76] Other programs have shown the potential benefits—including reduction of medical errors and increased hand hygiene—of including patients in safety initiatives, although various institutional factors may limit this potential (Davis et al., 2007;[77] Longtin et al., 2010;[78] Weingart et al., 2005,[79] 2011).[80] Using a different approach, initiatives at one healthcare organization, using value stream analysis and production system methods, improved care by incorporating patients in continuous improvement projects and measuring value from the patient perspective (Toussaint, 2009).[81] In one example, leaders at Dana-Farber Cancer

Institute invited patients and family members to populate all decision-making structures and processes in the organization. Patients provided input on organizational policies, were placed on continuous improvement teams, and were invited to join search committees and develop educational programming for staff (Ponte et al., 2003).[82] Leaders at the organizational level made the commitment to patient-centered care and communicated that vision to the organization (Shaller and The Commonwealth Fund, 2007).[83]

Another strategy for engaging patients in organizational change is routine measurement. The use of valid and reliable instruments can document the gaps between what routinely occurs and the ideal, thereby stimulating behavioral change among clinicians and patients. These tools include patient experience surveys, mechanisms for submitting complaints, and other feedback opportunities for patients. Beyond the information received, these tools convey the message that the voices of patients, families, and other caregivers are important (Shaller and The Commonwealth Fund, 2007).[84] Patient portals, dashboards, and other information technology-enabled devices are another avenue for bridging the gap between clinician visits and patients' ongoing information and health monitoring needs. By simplifying communication, email and telephone care allow patients to reach their clinicians easily and receive information when they need it. In one organization, office visits fell by 9 percent after the implementation of electronic health records that facilitated effective patient–clinician communication via telephone (Garrido et al., 2005).[85] Similarly, patient portals allow patients to communicate with their clinicians, access their health information, and monitor their own health, thereby facilitating their active participation in their care (Halamka et al., 2008;[86] Shaller and The Commonwealth Fund, 2007).[87] One example of the use of a patient portal in chronic care management is the Palo Alto Medical Foundation's diabetes management system, which allows patients and their clinicians to monitor key measures for the condition and highlights how the measures relate to overall health goals. Early focus group results indicate that while patients initially used the portal because they knew clinicians reviewed the results, over time they started using the system on their own to understand how different behaviors affected their health (IOM, 2011d).[88] Likewise, Partners HealthCare's Center for Connected Health provides health information technology for patients with cardiac conditions, diabetes and hypertension that allows them to share information with their clinicians and receive feedback. While some patients stop participating early on, 90% of those who remain active through the first two months continue to participate (IOM, 2011d).[89] These examples demonstrate the potential of health information technologies, as well as highlight the need for these technologies to be easy for patients to use and access.

Digital methods and tools physicians can use to inform, engage, involve and empower patients

Until recently, healthcare was characterized by an information asymmetry in which physicians served as the dominant source of medical information for patients. The Internet has rapidly transformed the health information landscape—initially opening up myriad resources, targeted to the general public, for health-related guidance and information, and then, with the emergence of Web 2.0, enabling the public to easily create and share health-related content online. Patients have responded to this shift by increasingly seeking health-related information outside of the care environment (Fox and Jones, 2009)[90] and creating and contributing to a wide variety of social networks and health websites (Sarasohn-Kahn, 2008).[91] Perhaps the most important opportunity that comes with greater information availability is the emergence of a culture that recognizes and supports the unique contributions of both patients and providers to care decisions and health management. Such a shift moves patient-centered care beyond a focus on "information, communication, and education of patients" (IOM, 2001)[92] to a system in which patients are engaged as full partners in their care and disease management.[93]

Effective use of health information technology (HIT) can drive significant improvements in physician and health system performance. A learning health system for patients places priority on meaningful applications of HIT to help patients gain access to their health data, relevant knowledge, and tools to guide self-care and health management. Shared information can help to create an effective partnership between the professional health team and patients in order to improve patients' health.

HIT has the big potential to transform the patient experience. Consider for example diabetes, it is a ravaging disease that is lived with by making hundreds of decisions, such as what to eat and whether to exercise, remembering to take their medications, checking their blood glucose, and so on. If patients are going to make the decisions that can keep their diabetes under control, they also must have good and timely information. Not surprisingly, as with physician performance improvement, patients benefit from the provision of real-time information more than from a physician critique three months after making a decision. Moreover, information must be understandable to patients and relevant to their individual health goals and concerns.

Thus, with the changing demands of consumers, the aging of the population, and incentives for quality improvement, how can HIT facilitate better healthcare outcomes at lower cost? Following are some of the main examples of approaches that might be adopted more widely with the growth of HIT.

Telemedicine: Seeks to improve a patient's health by permitting two-way, real time interactive communication between the patient, and the clinician at the distant site. Telemedicine may be as simple as two health professionals discussing a case over the telephone, or as complex as using satellite technology and video-conferencing equipment to conduct a real-time consultation between medical specialists in two different countries.

There are three main categories of telemedicine:

*   *Remote patient monitoring:* Allows patients with chronic diseases to be monitored in their homes through the use of devices that collect data about blood sugar levels, blood pressure or other vital signs. The data can be reviewed instantly by remote clinicians.
*   *Store and forward technology:* Stores clinical data, as well as X-rays and other images, and forwards the data to other locations for evaluation.
*   *Interactive telemedicine:* Allows clinicians and patients to communicate in real time. Such sessions can be conducted in the patient's home or in a nearby healthcare facility. Electronic provider visits hold the potential for enhancing patient– provider communication and enhancing the ability of primary care providers to offer care for non-urgent medical issues. Based on the results of the web Visit Study: Impact of Online Doctor-Patient Communication on Satisfaction and Cost of Care, conducted by researchers at Stanford and the University of California at Berkeley, physicians reported that the system was easy to use (72%), satisfying (53%), and preferable to an office visit for non-urgent care (56%). Analysis of health claim costs for the intervention group showed a statistically significant lower cost for office-based claims (p <0.01) and total claims (p <0.05) (Zimmerman et al.).[94] Research by the American Medical Association shows that roughly 1 billion doctor visits occur each year in the United States, and of those, 70% are unnecessary and could be avoided by consulting with a clinician by phone, email or text. Deloitte has estimated that within the next few years, one of every six patients will be seen virtually.

Electronic Health Record (EHR)

An EHR is an electronic version of a patient's medical history which can include demographics, progress notes, medications, vital signs, past medical history, laboratory data and radiology reports. The EHR automates access to information and has the potential to streamline the clinician's workflow. It also has the ability to support other care-related activities directly or indirectly through various interfaces, including evidence-based decision support, quality management and outcomes reporting.

Meaningful Use is a Medicare and Medicaid program in the US that awards incentives for using certified electronic health records to improve patient care. To achieve Meaningful Use and avoid penalties, providers must follow a set of criteria that serve as a roadmap for effectively using an EHR.

As part of the demonstration initiative Pursuing Perfection, a project of the Institute for Healthcare Improvement, participants from Whatcom County, Washington, decided to fully embrace the concept of patient-centered care by facilitating communication between chronically ill patients and their healthcare delivery system. With patients as part of the planning team, they developed the website *www.patientpowered.org*, which includes information on initiatives to improve patient-centeredness, as well as useful information and tools for self-management of chronic conditions. Part of the Patient Powered website is a shared care plan (SCP)—a document, either web-based or on paper, that allows patients to gather all their health-related information in one place. The document includes the patient's personal profile, healthcare team members, chronic and long-term diagnoses, self-management and lifestyle goals and action steps, treatment goals, names of prescriptions, medications and allergies, and advance directives. An SCP is designed to be much more user-friendly than a dense medical record, which typically is organized chronologically and fragments information by individual providers and locations. Patients can store the SCP information on paper or on a secure website linked to patientpowered.org and can upload information themselves or have other family members add vital information about their care. An evaluation of the implementation of the SCP through patientpowered.org in conjunction with a clinical care specialist (nurse or social worker) demonstrated increased patient satisfaction with clinical care and a cost savings of approximately $3,000 per year for enrolled patients (Safford).[95]

Until recently, it has been difficult for patients to gain access to their clinical information and medical records, and only rarely do they review the notes their clinicians write following encounters, both in the ambulatory setting and on hospital wards. Today, electronic health records (EHRs), coupled to patient-facing, secure Internet portals, facilitate access if providers decide to offer it. Some worry that general concern about loss of privacy may lead patients to withhold information or refrain from visiting doctors when care may be indicated. On the other hand, easy access to records may encourage underserved populations to engage more actively with the healthcare system. Overall, information gaps may be narrowed, thereby facilitating better continuity and integration of care. OpenNotes (http://www.myopennotes.org), a rapidly expanding national movement in the USA that encourages clinicians to offer patients ready access to their encounter notes, began as a demonstration and evaluation study in 2010, with 105 volunteer primary care physicians (PCPs) and 19,000 of their patients in Boston, rural Pennsylvania, and the Seattle inner city. Notified automatically via a secure email message when a note was signed, patients were invited to review their doctors' notes, and they were again encouraged to do so prior to a next scheduled visit. Results from the one-year evaluation were striking and attracted considerable attention from professional groups and consumers. Four of five patients read their note(s); two-thirds of those surveyed a year after the experiment started reported potentially important clinical benefits; 99% of the patients completing surveys wanted the practice to continue, whether or not they chose to read the notes; and 85% indicated that access would be important for their future choice of a provider or system. Perhaps most strikingly, at the end of the study, no doctor chose to discontinue the practice. Although percentages of patients reading their notes may differ, study results indicate that patients both value and benefit from online access to clinical notes, and adherence for some medications may indeed improve. Patients can read their notes at home or wherever they want, that is, asynchronously and repeatedly, and can readily share their notes with people of their choice by downloading them and forwarding them, or by inviting others to read them on a computer, tablet or smartphone.

Patient Portals

A Patient Portal is a secure and private web-based portal. It enables patients and healthcare professionals to exchange documents, images, results and messages. Patient Portals help patients become more involved in their care by helping to provide a clear understanding of what they need to do, which in turn can result in a better patient experience and improved health outcomes. A Patient Portal can empower and engage patients by:

- Providing secure access to their health information.
- Improving communication with their care providers.
- Helping them to take responsibility for their own health.
- Providing easy access to relevant and current reference information.

As part of the Meaningful Use Stage 2 requirements, healthcare providers in the US must have at least 5% of their patients using an online patient portal to get incentive payments.

Despite all those benefits, it's not always easy for practices to convince patients to use portals—or even to sign up in the first place. A recent study of 5,000

Americans found that just 20% were able to schedule medical appointments online and only 15% could email their doctor.

To boost adoption rates, it is critical to reinforce the value of the portal to patients, and provide them with specific training. A 2017 Athena Research study of nearly 600 primary care practices across the network evaluated how successful practices were in getting their patients to register for and engage with their portals. The *portal adoption rate* determines the percentage of patients who registered for the portal prior to, or within 30 days of, a visit with their doctor. *Portal usage rates* reflect the percentage who interacted with their portal within 30 days of a visit.

Researchers found that small practices—those with six or fewer physicians—had better portal adoption and usage rates than larger regional and national health systems. While small practices typically have the resources and close patient relationships to be able to engage their clients more fully, practices of any size can benefit from adopting a few simple steps to increase portal use among their patient populations. Here's what two practices with high adoption and usage rates are doing to engage patients on their portals:

1. *Make portals indispensable for both staff and patients:* Practices with high portal adoption and usage rates not only emphasize that the portal is the primary mode of communication for updates, lab results and appointments, they go as far as possible in making signup mandatory.
2. *Show and tell:* High-performing practices find that the real sticking power for portals comes from showing patients how easy and useful these tools are with a hands-on approach.
3. *Integrate the portal into each phase of the patient visit:* High-performing practices train staff members on every aspect of their portal, the first step to integrate the portal into each phase of a patient's visit, from check in to check out and beyond.
4. *Always improve:* Despite boasting high portal adoption and usage numbers, successful practices keep seeking out ways to improve the scope of the tool.

Combining these strategies helps practices take advantage of the portal's ability to save their time and energy, a welcome convenience in any setting where workloads are high.

As a last example, patients at Fargo Family Health Center decided they wanted to create a blog and listening service for patients living with diabetes. Instead of joining a public blog/support group for patients with diabetes, the patient advisers in the demonstration felt it was important that their providers know about their struggles and celebrations in living with diabetes. They also wanted to learn from other patients being treated at the health center. Patients registered for the site, and individual peer-to-peer phone calls were available for additional support. In the spirit of the phrase "all politics is local," patients decided to create a geographic and condition-specific community of support for themselves that could be accessed by their clinical providers. Technical issues such as security and sharing of clinical information were challenges for this team. However, the opportunity to create a local community of patients who could offer each other support, provide information to their clinical partners, and impact the care provided at the local level helped the team decide to take on these issues and find effective ways of managing concerns about privacy and security for their participants.

Mobile health

Mobile health, or mHealth, is defined as the delivery of healthcare services via mobile communication devices. It has the potential to address one of the most pressing global challenges: making healthcare more accessible, faster, better and cheaper. Unlike many other forms of communication mHealth will likely have a greater effect on how care is delivered for three reasons:

- Mobile devices are ubiquitous and personal.
- Competition will continue to drive lower pricing and increase functionality.
- Mobility by its very nature implies that users are always part of a network, which radically increases the variety, velocity, volume and value of information they send and receive.

The benefits of mHealth can be countless. For example, doctors can monitor the status of cancer patients receiving chemotherapy using the sensors in smartphones and an algorithm that detects worsening symptoms based on objective changes in patient behavior, according to a new study.[96] The findings indicate that worsening symptoms during cancer treatments can be detected using smartphones that patients likely already own and use. Real-time estimation of symptoms and side effects could provide an opportunity for doctors to intervene earlier between clinic visits, preventing unnecessary physician or hospital visits and improving patient quality of life.

Despite clear consensus from most stakeholders that mHealth has significant potential to support patient self-care and reduce the demand on healthcare systems, its use has yet to be mainstreamed—80% of apps are abandoned in two weeks. The EU's Green Paper on mHealth identified seven major areas of concern with mobile health apps that need to be addressed before the technology can go mainstream. These were:

1. the need for clarity on levels of data security to protect public and patients;
2. lack of appropriate governance of lifestyle (non-medical) health apps;
3. possible threats to patient safety;
4. lack of transparency about who lies behind an app;
5. lack of clinical input and integration with healthcare systems;
6. lack of clarity about whether health apps produce positive outcomes;
7. ill-funded nature of the entire enterprise that surrounds app development.

As anticipated, there is one key reason missing from the EU list: more often than not health apps are developed in isolation from their intended users: patients and the public (see Chapters 3 and 6).

We need devices that are easy to use and that promote ongoing customer engagement. Developers must take the time to explore and understand the EHR vendor's API. Mobile health tools and technologies must integrate into the existing healthcare environment in a cost-effective and timely manner.

Wearable technologies

The terms "wearable technology," "wearable devices," and "wearables" all refer to electronic technologies or computers that are incorporated into items of clothing and accessories which can be worn on the body. These wearable devices can perform many of the same computing tasks as mobile phones and laptop computers

With wearable technology, learning more about yourself has not only become high tech but also real-time. From devices and apps that help you track heart rate and food consumption details to gadgets that monitor your mood and even surrounding air, the "quantified self" is a reality for the everyday person.

What's exciting about wearables and wireless monitoring devices is their potential to empower consumers to make meaningful changes and improvements to their health, on their own. What's more, the current generation of wearables can empower those with chronic conditions to better monitor and manage their conditions. It has been estimated the wearable technology industry will see a fivefold increase over the next ten years, from over $14 billion to over $70 billion

Social media

Social media allows healthcare providers to connect and engage directly with thousands of people and organizations, be seen to understand and take on board their viewpoints and involve them in local solutions. It also allows them to reply to questions and comments and, in some cases, challenge misinformation. This creates a much more transparent and healthy environment for debate and discussion. Social media in healthcare changes the traditional one-to-one patient–doctor dialog to one-to-many and many-to-many dialogs between doctors and patients, patients and patients and doctors and doctors at a phenomenal speed. This fundamental change in how people in the healthcare ecosystem interact with each other opens up the possibilities for many novel applications of social media in healthcare such as:

- Patients and doctors interact via social media to promote awareness about diseases, precautions and other health-related information with each other.
- Patients use social media to meet their health-related wants, needs and preferences.
- Online applications like WebMD offer platforms for both consumer and clinician moderated health-related conversations.
- Clinical investigators and research organizations use online communities to recruit volunteers for clinical trials.
- Public health and regulatory agencies use social media tools for public health campaigns and announcements.
- Web applications are used for treatment, clinician and hospital selection comparisons.

Pitfalls and promises of patient portals and health applications

As a secure online website providing patients access to their health information, the portal aims to improve quality of care by engaging patients as active participants in their care. While portal functions vary, most allow patients to view laboratory test results, immunizations, medications and allergies, as well as to send secure messages to their physician.[14] However, the portal can be difficult to navigate, and patients may struggle to understand their medical information. A recent systematic review of patient and provider attitudes toward patient portal use found that the most negatively perceived feature was user-friendliness, making the portal difficult to navigate. Addressing these issues may help improve patient-centered care.

On the other hand and for a different engagement purpose, several companies have designed and created various tracking applications to encourage people to actively participate in their health. Applications, such as Mango Health (San Francisco, CA), Fitbit (San Francisco, CA), and Apple (Cupertino, CA) iPhone 6's built in Health app, have consumer-friendly features with easy login access, real-time tracking, and simplified data display. From a patient standpoint, these features likely make the applications more intuitive and easy to use than patient portals. Furthermore, mHealth apps live on mobile devices, which make them easily accessible with little effort to login after setting up the account. This ubiquitous access is one of the reasons mobile technology is rapidly replacing desktop technologies.

Although apps might serve a different purpose, patient portals could adopt certain app features that lead to better engagement success with patients. While it is not clear if apps influence patient behavior, condition-specific apps may help patients improve outcomes. Nevertheless, mHealth apps' features and functionality do not extend widely to provide users access to their institutionally generated health data. At this point we also do not really know the value of the data generated by mHealth apps, and researchers are still determining how to best use the data from new apps like ResearchKit. These apps are also not heavily regulated and could contain poor quality or incorrect information, and some apps have been found to produce incorrect or inconsistent data. Despite increasing use of mHealth apps, up to 80% of apps are abandoned after only two weeks, suggesting more research is needed to understand what features engender longevity. Additionally, a recent study regarding health app use among *vulnerable populations* found that participants lacked confidence with the technology and expressed frustration with design and navigation. The authors called for participatory design, testing and training with diverse patient populations to improve use (see Chapters 3 and Chapter 6).

While mobile apps may offer more personalized interactions, it has been suggested that these apps need to be connected to *personal health records* to be effective and improve patient outcomes. However, there are legal concerns related to data protection and some uncertainty as to when and if mHealth apps fall under HIPAA or a developer's own privacy policy, if available. Thus a great deal of attention and focus must be paid to the development and distribution of health apps which are truly useful, relevant, credible and accurate, as well as to the way they are used by patients and healthcare professionals.

Empowerment and artificial intelligence

Artificial intelligence (AI), the power of a machine to copy intelligent human behavior, is aggressively entering the healthcare space and is expected to have profound effects on the way medicine is practiced.

If effectively developed and implemented with a great deal of attention on ethics, one of the best impacts of AI will be making healthcare more patient-centered by reducing or, sometimes, eliminating the exclusive reliance on doctors' imperfect memory and partial knowledge, and recover some precious time by using machine-generated information to work with patients and shape their specific treatment.

For example, AI could organize patient journeys or treatment plans more effectively, as well as offer physicians with basically all the insights they need to make better decisions for their patients and the overall healthcare system.

Following are some of the main applications of AI aiming at improving patient empowerment:

1. *Mining medical records:* The most obvious application of artificial intelligence in healthcare is data management (see Chapter 5).
2. *Designing treatment plans:* IBM Watson, for example, is able to provide clinicians evidence-based treatment options.
3. *Assisting repetitive jobs:* Medical Sieve, a new algorithm from IBM, is an ambitious long-term exploratory project to build the next generation "cognitive assistant" with analytical, reasoning capabilities and a wide range of clinical knowledge.
4. *Getting the most out of in-person and online consultations:* Babylon, the British online medical consultation service, offers medical AI consultation based on personal medical history and common medical knowledge. Users report their symptoms to the app, which assesses them against a database of diseases using speech recognition. After analyzing each patient's history and prognosis, Babylon offers a suitable course of action. The app also reminds patients to take their medication, and follow up on how they're feeling.
5. *Health assistance and medication management:* Molly, the first virtual nurse developed by the medical start-up Sense.ly, has an exclusive purpose to help patients to better monitor their disease and treatment. The interface uses machine learning to support patients with chronic conditions between doctors' visits. It provides customized monitoring and follow-up care, with a strong focus on chronic diseases.
6. *Improving compliance:* The AiCure app, supported by The National Institutes of Health, uses a smartphone's webcam and AI to autonomously confirm that patients are adhering to their prescriptions, or with better terms, supporting them to make sure they know how to manage their condition.

Indeed, the use of AI may hide a number of pitfalls, mostly for a peculiar and sensitive area such as healthcare. The following are some main precautions we must take in addition to all the steps (already covered in the previous chapters) we need to make for a health digital tool to be successfully adopted by physicians and patients and create value:

- Development and disclosure of *ethical standards* which are applicable to and mandatory for healthcare stakeholders.
- *Gradual introduction* of AI solutions in order to identify strengths and weaknesses and make appropriate adjustments before expanded introduction.
- *Healthcare providers' education and training* should provide basic knowledge and involve them in on the job training programs aimed at providing them the needed knowledge and skills to use AI solutions in their clinical practice.
- *Patients' education and training* should help patients value the benefits of AI in their disease management and become familiar with AI tools

> "Traditional as well as digital tools need to be integrated and used to successfully pursue patient empowerment."

Notes

1 Peter Rieckmann et al. (2015), "Achieving patient engagement in multiple sclerosis: A perspective from the multiple sclerosis in the 21st Century Steering Group." *Multiple Sclerosis and Related Disorders*, 4, 202–218.
2 Marie-Christine R. Goodworth et al. (2014), "Variables associated with patient activation in persons with multiple sclerosis." *Journal of Health Psychology*, 21(1), 82–92.
3 R.E. Davis, R. Jacklin, N. Sevdalis, and C.A. Vincent (2007), "Patient involvement in patient safety: what factors influence patient participation and engagement?" *Health Expect*, 10, 259–267.
4 Antoinette von Pückler (2013), "A patient's perspective of partnership in the treatment of multiple sclerosis: MS regimes—An orchestrated approach." *Journal of the Neurological Sciences*, 335(1–2), 1–4, https://doi.org/10.1016/j.jns.2013.08.025.
5 F.D. Duffy, G.H. Gordon, G. Whelan, et al. (2004), "Assessing competence in communication and interpersonal skills: The Kalamazoo II report." *Acad Med: J Assoc Am Med Coll*, 79, 495–507.
6 A. Coulter (2005), "What do patients and the public want from primary care?" *BMJ* 331,1199. doi:https://doi.org/10.1136/bmj.331.7526.1199
7 N.L. Keating, D.C. Green, A.C. Kao, et al. (2002), *J Gen Intern Med*. 17, 29. https://doi.org/10.1046/j.1525-1497.2002.10209.x.
8 Paul Little et al. (2001), "Observational study of effect of patient centredness and positive approach on outcomes of general practice consultations." *BMJ*, 323, 908.
9 A. Solari (2014), "Effective communication at the point of multiple sclerosis diagnosis." *Multiple Sclerosis Journal*, 20(4), 397–402. https://doi.org/10.1177/1352458514523061.
10 S. Shea (2006), *Improving Medication Adherence: How to Talk to Patients about Their Medications*. Philadelphia, PA: Wolters Kluwer Health.
11 The Adopt One! Challenge website: http://mindthegap.smarthealthmessaging.com/2013/08/13/the-adopt-one-challenge-the-first-step-to-better-patient-engagement-patient-experiences-2/.

12 Continuous Care for Health website: https://www.continuouscare.io/.

13 Robert M. Anderson et al. (2010), "Patient empowerment: Myths and misconceptions." *Patient Education and Counseling*, 79(3), 277–282. [online]. Available at www.pec-journal. com/article/S0738-3991(09)00327-9/fulltext [Accessed March 13, 2018].

14 Robert M. Anderson et al. (2010), "Patient empowerment: Myths and misconceptions." *Patient Education and Counseling*, 79(3), 277–282. [online]. Available at www.pec-journal. com/article/S0738-3991(09)00327-9/fulltext [Accessed March 13, 2018].

15 S. Rollnick, W.R. Miller, and C.C. Butler (2007), *Motivational Interviewing in Health Care: Helping Patients Change Behavior* (Applications of Motivational Interviewing). London: The Guilford Press.

16 There is also a need for research on interventions that can improve a patient's ability to manage health information (Berkman et al., 2011).

17 Some interventions to remedy this limitation are straightforward; one study found that simply asking patients whether there was "something else" to discuss instead of "anything else" reduced the number of unmet concerns by almost 80 percent (Heritage et al., 2007).

18 B.A. Golomb, M.A. Evans (2008), "Statin adverse effects: A review of the literature and evidence for a mitochondrial mechanism." *American Journal of Cardiovascular Drugs: Drugs, Devices, and Other Interventions*, 8 (6), 373–418.

19 M. Maurer, P. Dardess, K.L. Carman, K. Frazier, and L. Smeeding (2012), *Guide to Patient and Family Engagement: Environmental Scan Report*. Rockville, MD: Agency for Healthcare Research and Quality.

20 W. Levinson, C.S. Lesser, and R.M. Epstein (2010), "Developing physician communication skills for patient-centered care." *Health Affairs* 7, 1310–1318.

21 P. Kinnersley, A. Edwards, K. Hood, N. Cadbury, R. Ryan, H. Prout, D. Owen, F. MacBeth, P. Butow, and C. Butler (2007), "Interventions before consultations for helping patients address their information needs." *Cochrane Database Systematic Reviews*, 3.

22 A. Coulter and J. Ellins (2006), Patient-focused interventions: A review of the evidence. [online]. Available at www.health.org.uk/publications/research_reports/patientfocused .html (Accessed March 13, 2018].

23 IOM (2004), *Health Literacy: A Prescription to End Confusion*. Washington, DC: The National Academies Press.

24 Committee on Improving the Quality of Cancer Care (2013), Addressing the Challenges of an Aging Population; Board on Health Care Services; Institute of Medicine; L. Levit, E. Balogh, S. Nass et al., editors. Delivering High-Quality Cancer Care: Charting a New Course for a System in Crisis. Washington (DC): National Academies Press (US); 2013 Dec 27. 3, Patient-Centered Communication and Shared Decision Making. [online]. Available at https://www.ncbi.nlm.nih.gov/books/NBK202146/ [Accessed March 20, 2018].

25 E.D. Collins, C.P. Moore, K.F. Clay, S.A. Kearing, A.M. O'Connor, H.A. Llewellyn-Thomas, J.R.J. Barth, and K.R. Sepucha (2009), "Can women with early-stage breast cancer make an informed decision for mastectomy." *Journal of Clinical Oncology*, 27(4), 519–525.

26 D.E. Arterburn, E.O. Westbrook, T.A. Bogart, K.R. Sepucha, S.N. Bock, and W.G. Weppner (2011), "Randomized trial of a video-based patient decision aid for bariatric surgery." *Obesity* (Silver Spring), 8(19), 1669–1675.

27 J.K. Belkora, A. Teng, S. Volz, M.K. Loth, L.J. Esserman (2011), "Expanding the reach of decision and communication aids in a breast care center: A quality improvement study." *Patient Education and Counseling*, 83(2), 234–239.

28 A.M. O'Connor, H.A. Llewellyn-Thomas, and A.B. Flood (2004), "Modifying unwarranted variations in health care: Shared decision making using patient decision aids." *Health Affairs (Millwood)*. Suppl. Variation, VAR63–72.

29 A.M. O'Connor, D.S. Tacey, M.J. Barry, N.F Col, K.B. Eden, V. Entwistle, V. Fiset, M. Holmes-Rovner, S. Khangura, H. Llewellyn-Thomas, and D.R. Rovner (2007a), "Do patient decision aids meet effectiveness criteria of the international patient decision aid standards collaboration? A systematic review and meta-analysis." *Medical Decision Making*, 5(27), 554–574.

30 L.I. Solberg, S.E. Asche, K. Sepucha, N.M. Thygeson, J.E. Madden, L. Morrissey, K.K. Kraemer, L.H. Anderson (2010), "Informed choice assistance for women making uterine fibroid treatment decisions: A practical clinical trial." *Medical Decision Making*, 4(30), 444–452.

31 D. Stacey, C.L. Bennett, M.J. Barry, N.F. Col, K.B. Eden, M. Holmes-Rovner, H. Llewellyn-Thomas, A. Lyddiatt, F. Legare, and R. Thomson (2011), "Decision aids for people facing health treatment or screening decisions." *Cochrane Database of Systematic Reviews*, 10, CD001431.

32 L.F. Degner, L.J. Kristjanson, D. Bowman, J.A. Sloan, K.C. Carriere, J.O'Neil, B. Bilodeau, P. Watson, and B. Mueller (1997), "Information needs and decisional preferences in women with breast cancer." *Journal of the American Medical Association*, 18(277), 1485–1492.

33 G.S. Chung, R.E. Lawrence, F.A. Curlin, V. Arora, D.O. Meltzer (2011), "Predictors of hospitalised patients' preferences for physician-directed medical decision-making." *Journal of Medical Ethics*, 2(38), 77–82.

34 R.B. Deber, N. Kraetschmer, S. Urowitz, and N. Sharpe (2007), "Do people want to be autonomous patients? Preferred roles in treatment decision-making in several patient populations." *Health Expectations*, 3(10), 248–258.

35 H. Fineberg (2012), "From shared decision making to patient-centered decision making." *Israel Journal of Health Policy Research*, 1(1), 6.

36 W. Levinson, A. Kao, and A. Kuby, RA. (2005), "Not all patients want to participate in decision making: A national study of public preferences." *Thisted Journal of General Internal Medicine*, 6(20), 531–535.

37 L.I. Solberg, S.E. Asche, L.H. Anderson, K. Sepucha, N.M. Thygeson, J.E. Madden, L. Morrissey, and K.K. Kraemer (2009), "Evaluating preference-sensitive care for uterine fibroids: It's not so simple." *Journal of Women's Health*, 7(18), 1071–1079.

38 R.M. Epstein, R.L. Street (2007), *Patient-centered communication in cancer care: Promoting healing and reducing suffering*. National Cancer Institute. NIH Publication No. 07-6225.

39 R.M. Epstein, R.L. Street (2007), *Patient-centered communication in cancer care: Promoting healing and reducing suffering*. National Cancer Institute. NIH Publication No. 07-6225.

40 R.M. Epstein, R.L. Street (2007), *Patient-centered communication in cancer care: Promoting healing and reducing suffering*. National Cancer Institute. NIH Publication No. 07-6225.

41 R.M. Epstein, R.L. Street (2007), *Patient-centered communication in cancer care: Promoting healing and reducing suffering*. National Cancer Institute. NIH Publication No. 07-6225.

42 T. Porter-O'Grady and K. Malloch (2007), *Quantum Leadership: A Resource for Healthcare Innovation*, 2nd edition. Sudbury, MA: Jones and Bartlett Publishers.

43 J.O. Busari (2013), "The discourse of generational segmentation and the implications for postgraduate medical education." (Perspectives on Medical Education). [online]. Available at https://www.ncbi.nlm.nih.gov/pmc/articles/PMC3824753/ (Accessed March 20, 2018].

44 D.L. Frosch, S.G. May, K.A. Rendle, C. Tietbohl, and G. Elwyn (2012), "Authoritarian physicians and patients' fear of being labeled 'difficult' among key obstacles to shared decision making." *Health Affairs (Millwood)*, 31(5), 1030–1038.

45 R.M. Epstein, R.L. Street (2007), *Patient-centered communication in cancer care: Promoting healing and reducing suffering*. National Cancer Institute. NIH Publication No. 07-6225.

46 R.M. Epstein, R.L. Street (2007), *Patient-centered communication in cancer care: Promoting healing and reducing suffering*. National Cancer Institute. NIH Publication No. 07-6225.

47 IOM (2011a), *Clinical Practice Guidelines We Can Trust*. Washington, DC: The National Academies Press.

48 R.M. Epstein, R.L. Street (2007), *Patient-centered communication in cancer care: Promoting healing and reducing suffering*. National Cancer Institute. NIH Publication No. 07-6225.

49 IOM (2008a), *Cancer Care for the Whole Patient: Meeting Psychosocial Health Needs*. Washington, DC: The National Academies Press.

50 J.W. Mack and T.J. Smith (2012), "Reasons why physicians do not have discussions about poor prognosis, why it matters, and what can be improved." *Journal of Clinical Oncology*, 30(22), 2715–2117.

51 R.M. Epstein, R.L. Street (2007), *Patient-centered communication in cancer care: Promoting healing and reducing suffering*. National Cancer Institute. NIH Publication No. 07-6225.

52 IOM (2008a), *Cancer Care for the Whole Patient: Meeting Psychosocial Health Needs*. Washington, DC: The National Academies Press.

53 E.D. Collins, C.P. Moore, K.F. Clay, S.A. Kearing, A.M. O'Connor, H.A. Llewellyn-Thomas, J.R.J. Barth, and K.R. Sepucha (2009), "Can women with early-stage breast cancer make an informed decision for mastectomy." *Journal of Clinical Oncology*, 27(4), 519–525.

54 A. Berman (2012), "Living life in my own way—and dying that way as well." *Health Affairs (Millwood)*, 31(4), 871–874.

55 IOM (2011a), *Clinical Practice Guidelines We Can Trust*. Washington, DC: The National Academies Press.

56 R. Matsuyama, S. Reddy, and T.J. Smith (2006), "Why do patients choose chemotherapy near the end of life? A review of the perspective of those facing death from cancer." *Journal of Clinical Oncology*, 24(21), 3490–3496.

57 A. Surbone (2010), "Cultural competence in oncology: Where do we stand?" *Annals of Oncology*, 21(1), 3–5.

58 A. Surbone (2010), "Cultural competence in oncology: Where do we stand?" *Annals of Oncology*, 21(1), 3–5.

59 R.M. Epstein and R.L. Street (2007), *Patient-Centered Communication in Cancer Care: Promoting Healing and Reducing Suffering*. National Cancer Institute. NIH Publication No. 07-6225.

60 IOM and NRC (National Research Council) (1999), *Ensuring Quality Cancer Care*. Washington, DC: National Academy Press.

61 R.M. Epstein and R.L. Street (2007), *Patient-Centered Communication in Cancer Care: Promoting Healing and Reducing Suffering*. National Cancer Institute. NIH Publication No. 07-6225.

62 J.C. Gruman (2013), "An accidental tourist finds her way in the dangerous land of serious illness." *Health Affairs (Millwood)*, 32(2), 427–431.

63 IOM (2011a), *Clinical Practice Guidelines We Can Trust*. Washington, DC: The National Academies Press.

64 Committee on Improving the Quality of Cancer Care (2013), Addressing the Challenges of an Aging Population; Board on Health Care Services; Institute of Medicine; L. Levit, E. Balogh, S. Nass et al., editors. Delivering High-Quality Cancer Care: Charting a New Course for a System in Crisis. Washington (DC): National Academies Press (US); 2013 Dec 27. 3, Patient-Centered Communication and Shared Decision Making. [online]. Available at https://www.ncbi.nlm.nih.gov/books/NBK202146/ [Accessed May 30 2018].

65 Institute of Medicine (IOM) (2013). *Best Care at Lower Cost: The Path to Continuously Learning Health Care in America*. Washington, DC: The National Academies Press. https://doi.org/10.17226/13444.

66 B. Balik, J. Conway, L. Zipperer, and J. Watson (2011), "Achieving an Exceptional Patient and Family Experience of Inpatient Hospital Care." IhI Innovation Series white paper. Cambridge, MA: Institute for healthcare Improvement.

67 M. Maurer, P. Dardess, K.L. Carman, K. Frazier, and L. Smeeding (2012), "Guide to patient and family engagement: Environmental scan report." (Prepared by American Institutes for Research under contract HHSA 290-200-600019). AHRQ Publication No. 12-0042-EF. Rockville, MD: Agency for Healthcare Research and Quality.

68 S.C. Bergeson and J.D. Dean (2006), "A systems approach to patient-centered care." *JAMA*, 296(23), 2848–2451. PMID:17179462; DOI: 10.1001/jama.296.23.2848.

69 O. Groene (2011), "Patient centredness and quality improvement efforts in hospitals: rationale, measurement, implementation." *Int J Qual Health Care*, 23(5), 531–537. doi:10.1093/intqhc/mzr058.

70 B. Johnson, M. Abraham, J. Conway, L. Simmons, S. Edgman-Levitan, P. Sodomka, J. Schlucter, and D. Ford (2008), *Partnering with Patients and Families to Design a Patient- and Family-Centered Health Care System: Recommendations and Promising Practices.* Bethesda, MD: Institute for Family-Centered Care and Institute for Healthcare Improvement.

71 S.H. Scholle, P. Torda, D. Peikes, E. Han, and J. Genevro (2010), *Engaging Patients and Families in the Medical Home* (prepared by Mathematica Policy Research under contract no. HHSA290200900019i to2). Rockville, MD: Agency for Healthcare Research and Quality.

72 E. Litvak, and M. Bisognano (2011). More patients, less payment: Increasing hospital efficiency in the aftermath of health reform. Health Affairs (Millwood) 30(1):76–80.

73 E. Litvak, P.I. Buerhaus, F. Davidoff, M.C. Long, M.L. McManus, and D.M. Berwick (2005), "Managing unnecessary variability in patient demand to reduce nursing stress and improve patient safety." *Joint Commission Journal on Quality and Patient Safety*, 31(6), 330–338.

74 B. Balik, J. Conway, L. Zipperer, and J. Watson (2011), *Achieving an Exceptional Patient and Family Experience of Inpatient Hospital Care.* Cambridge, MA: Institute for Healthcare Improvement.

75 J. Conway, B. Johnson, S. Edgman-Levitan, J. Schlucter, D. Ford, P. Sodomka, and L. Simmons (2006), *Partnering with Patients and Families to Design a patient- and Family Centered Health Care System.* Bethesda, MD: Institute for Family-Centered Care with Institute for Healthcare Improvement.

76 P.R. Ponte, G. Conlin, J.B. Conway, S. Grant, C. Medeiros, J. Nies, L. Shulman, P. Branowicki, and K. Conley (2003), "Making patient-centered care come alive: Achieving full integration of the patient's perspective." *Journal of Nursing Administration*, 33(2), 82–90.

77 R.E. Davis, R. Jacklin, N. Sevdalis, and C.A. Vincent. 2007. "Patient involvement in patient safety: What factors influence patient participation and engagement?" *Health Expectations*, 10(3), 259–267.

78 Y. Longtin, H. Sax, L.L. Leape, S.E. Sheridan, L. Donaldson, and D. Pittet (2010), "Patient participation: Current knowledge and applicability to patient safety." *Mayo Clinic Proceedings*, 85(1), 53–62.

79 S.N. Weingart, O. Pagovich, D.Z. Sands, J.M. Li, M.D. Aronson, R.B. Davis, D.W. Bates, and R.S. Phillips (2005), "What can hospitalized patients tell us about adverse events? Learning from patient-reported incidents." *Journal of General Internal Medicine*, 20(9), 830–836.

80 S.N. Weingart, J. Zhu, L. Chiappetta, S.O. Stuver, E.C. Schneider, A.M. Epstein, J.A. David-Kasdan, C.L. Annas, F.J. Fowler, Jr., and J.S. Weissman (2011), "Hospitalized patients' participation and its impact on quality of care and patient safety." *International Journal for Quality in Health Care*, 23(3), 269–277.

81 J. Toussaint (2009), "Writing the new playbook for U.S. health care: Lessons from Wisconsin." *Health Affairs (Millwood)*, 28(5), 1343–1350.

82 P.R. Ponte, G. Conlin, J.B. Conway, S. Grant, C. Medeiros, J. Nies, L. Shulman, P. Branowicki, and K. Conley (2003), "Making patient-centered care come alive:

Achieving full integration of the patient's perspective." *Journal of Nursing Administration*, 33(2), 82–90.

83 D. Shaller, "Patient-Centered Care: What Does It Take?" The Commonwealth Fund, October 2007. [online]. Available at https://www.commonwealthfund.org/publications/fund-reports/2007/oct/patient-centered-care-what-does-it-take [Accessed March 30, 2018].

84 D. Shaller, "Patient-Centered Care: What Does It Take?" The Commonwealth Fund, October 2007. [online]. Available at https://www.commonwealthfund.org/publications/fund-reports/2007/oct/patient-centered-care-what-does-it-take [Accessed March 30, 2018].

85 T. Garrido, L. Jamieson, Y. Zhou, A. Wiesenthal, and L. Liang (2005), "Effect of electronic health records in ambulatory care: Retrospective, serial, cross sectional study." *British Medical Journal*, 330(7491), 581.

86 J.D. Halamka, K.D. Mandl, and P.C. Tang (2008), "Early experiences with personal health records." *Journal of the American Medical Informatics Association*, 15(1), 1–7.

87 D. Shaller, "Patient-Centered Care: What Does It Take?" The Commonwealth Fund, October 2007. [online]. Available at https://www.commonwealthfund.org/publications/fund-reports/2007/oct/patient-centered-care-what-does-it-take [Accessed March 30, 2018].

88 IOM (2011d), *Patients Charting the Course: Citizen Engagement in the Learning Health System: Workshop Summary*. Washington, DC: The National Academies Press.

89 IOM (2011d), *Patients Charting the Course: Citizen Engagement in the Learning Health System: Workshop Summary*. Washington, DC: The National Academies Press.

90 S. Fox and S. Jones (2009), "The social life of health information." [online]. Available at www.pewinternet.org/Reports/2009/8-the-social-life-of-health-information. [Accessed March 30 2018].

91 J. Sarasohn-Kahn (2008), "Reaching patients in a Health 2.0 world." *Marketing Health Services*, 28(3), 43.

92 IOM (2001) *Crossing the Quality Chasm: A New Health System for the 21st Century*. Washington, DC: National Academy Press.

93 Institute of Medicine (IOM) (2011), *Patients Charting the Course: Citizen Engagement and the Learning Health System: Workshop summary*. Washington, DC: The National Academies Press, p. 137. [online]. Available at https://www.ncbi.nlm.nih.gov/books/NBK91496/pdf/Bookshelf_NBK91496.pdf [Accessed March 20, 2018].

94 Institute of Medicine (IOM) 2011. *Patients Charting the Course: Citizen Engagement and the Learning Health System: Workshop Summary*. Washington, DC: The National Academies Press. https://doi.org/10.17226/12848.

95 B. Safford, "Pursuing perfection: Report from Whatcom county." Washington on patient-centered care. [online] Available at www.ihi.org/resources/Pages/ImprovementStories/PursuingPerfectionReportfromWhatcomCountyWashington-onPatientCenteredCare.aspx [Accessed March 20 2018]

96 Wendy Zellner (2017), "Smartphones let docs remotely monitor chemo patients." *Health and Medicine*. [online]. Available at https://www.futurity.org/smartphones-chemotherapy-cancer-1642712-2/ [Accessed March 20, 2018].

Creating the right setting to promote physicians' empowerment **9**

From the mindset of healthcare professionals to the lack of an internal protocol, training and data security, barriers to the adoption of health digital tools abound.

In this chapter we'll explore successful approaches to develop and implement an empowering internal healthcare environment.

We'll begin our journey with a **leading case history** on creating the right setting to promote physicians empowerment in action at the Mayo Clinic.

In a time when healthcare executives are challenged by increasing price competition, narrowing of insurance networks, and a greater proportion of patients with noncommercial insurance (e.g., Medicare, Medicaid) due to the Affordable Care resulting in declining reimbursements and, in parallel, by the large capital expenditures and dramatic increase of clerical burden for staff generated by the requirements for "meaningful use" of electronic health records, Mayo Clinic executives in addition to checking on external threats are also focused on equally important internal threats to organizational health. Motivated by the strong belief that successfully navigating the external challenges requires not only tremendous leadership but also committed and productive physicians working in partnership with leaders, Mayo Clinic executives have successfully implemented the following nine inexpensive strategies to prevent burnout and improve physician engagement:[1,2]

1. **Acknowledge and assess the problem:** The organization provides many opportunities for physicians to talk about the problems they face via different formats, including town halls, radio broadcasts, face-to-face meetings and video interviews.

2. **Identify and train physician leaders:** healthcare leaders look for physicians' leaders who have the ability to listen to, engage, develop and lead physicians. It is critical, though, that the organization help develop and train them.

3. **Develop and implement targeted interventions:** Three years ago Mayo identified departments that had burnout rates higher than the national average. To address the problem, administrators involved medical staff in engaging discussions about the problems and how the organization might make changes to help improve satisfaction. This prevented Mayo physicians from falling in the "victimhood" spiral while making them feel empowered to work with leaders to make necessary changes.

4. **Cultivate community at work:** Physicians at Mayo can gather in a dedicated meeting area stocked with fruit and beverages. Pursuing its commitment to cultivate a string sense of community, the organization has also experimented with small group meetings and a pilot program in which doctors shared meals at a local restaurant every two weeks. All these initiatives contributed to make it easier for physicians discuss the ups and downs of their clinical practice.

5. **Use rewards and incentives wisely:** Some physicians are motivated by financial rewards, but that can backfire if the model provides room for doctors to overwork, thus leading to more burnout.

6. John H. Noseworthy, M.D., president and CEO of Mayo Clinic, and Tait D. Shanafelt, director of the program on physician well-being, suggest that organizations consider **salaried compensation models** or rewards that offer more flexibility and time for physicians to follow aspects of work most meaningful to them.

7. **Align values and strengthen culture:** Mayo uses an all-staff survey to evaluate how well the organization meets its values. When the 2011 results came back that physicians thought the organization was less committed to staff, leaders established a task force to identify what went wrong. The group worked with physicians and senior leaders to determine areas for improvement, and the document is used to this day for recruitment and onboarding.

8. **Promote flexibility and work-life integration:** Many doctors work more than 60 hours per week, and the demands make it difficult for physicians to have a personal life. Organizations can help by offering physicians flexible work schedules, so they can start the workday earlier or later or work longer hours certain days a week so they can leave earlier on other days.

9. **Provide resources to promote resilience and self-care:** Noseworthy and Shanafelt suggest that organizations give individual physicians the necessary resources and training in skills to promote resilience. These tools must address work-life integration, fitness, sleep, diet, relationships and hobbies.

10. **Support evidence-based strategies that promote physician empowerment:** Mayo launched a program on physician well-being in 2007 to develop benchmarks to help reduce burnout.

As healthcare systems advance toward new digital care models, the key to success is physician empowerment, which must be promoted early and at the highest levels. Having empowered physicians makes it easier for organizations to implement critical programs and new initiatives. When physicians are fully empowered, an environment of trust and a genuine sense of value can be established. For example, physicians will have a stronger ability to practice at the top of their specialty and foster higher collegiality and collaboration. Ultimately, that is good for patients as well.

A survey conducted in 2011 by McKinsey & Company reveals that more than 70% of the physicians interviewed would make changes to their clinical practice, make greater use of evidence-based medicine, increase reporting of quality and outcomes metrics, or improve cost-saving efforts over the next few years.[3] Approximately 85% said they would be willing to make changes to the way they worked, or collaborate with other physicians to decrease waste and improve efficiencies. However, less than 20% of them said they had actually started any initiatives to meet their goals.

As highlighted many times in the previous chapters, physician attitudes are the key barriers to the transformation of the healthcare market—and the study notes physicians either don't believe they have much control over wasteful practices, or they believe they are not equipped to implement changes.

The study suggests that improving physician empowerment requires communicating the value of the change being initiated, establishing role models and utilizing peer review for motivation, training physicians on the impact of their day-to-day clinical decisions, and compensation and corporate structures that support physician efforts.

Best ways to empower physicians

Today, we see a great deal of discussion around financial benefits as a reason to get physicians engaged. But, surveys show that if the change is only a cost benefit to the hospital, there is less interest from physicians. This cost benefit approach doesn't drive engagement and the consequent empowerment or change physician behavior.[4]

Similar to the stages of angst, there are also stages of engagement. Generally, physicians either don't like change (aversion), or are okay with the change but not really enthusiastic about it (apathy). Finally, only after a lot of education and when they can see the value, does commitment to the change occur (engaged).

So what can healthcare organizations do to deepen the engagement of physicians?

First, physicians must believe the hospital can be trusted to consistently deliver on its commitments, such as promising to make operating room slots available so that surgeons can perform surgeries in a timely fashion. Even when apparently simple things such as dedicating a space for physicians to gather is achieved, trust is built between the hospital and the clinician. Physicians must also believe the hospital practices integrity and they will always be treated fairly with satisfactory solution to the problems which may occur. Physicians want to feel good about using the hospital and want to be sure that hospital use reflects positively upon them. This translates to having the hospital create services to support the delivery of exceptional patient care. Physicians are passionate about caring for their patients. They view the hospital as irreplaceable and an integral part of their lives and their practice of medicine. When hospitals focus too much on the bottom line and cut services, physicians may no longer feel that the hospital is irreplaceable or functions as an integral part of their practice.

Max Weber, a German sociologist, described four motivations that drive social action (that is, action in response to others' behavior) by motivating and driving people to change. Adapted for healthcare professionals, these are shared purpose, self-interest, respect and tradition. Leaders can use these levers to earn doctors' buy-in and generate the change the system so urgently needs. Indeed, in order for leaders to successfully engage and empower physicians, they must implement these four levers together, not in isolation.[5]

1. Setting, clarifying and sharing the goal

The idea of setting, clarifying and sharing the goal cannot be understated. The absolute goal of a physician is to care for patients and improve their quality of life. This ought to be the primary focus of any activity hospitals or other healthcare organizations do to engage physicians.

Indeed, in the new healthcare landscape, physicians' engagement must be part of a long-term strategy aiming at creating patient value and outcomes and reducing costs (see Chapter 3). To make engagement happen leaders must clarify what, exactly, they expect physicians engage with.

2. Shared purpose

To help physicians overcome their angst and resentment about what they might be losing as a result of the healthcare transformation, leaders must develop and share a clear vision of what they should expect on the other side of the chaos ahead: a better, perhaps even great, healthcare for patients. Improved patient care must be the essence and key priority of any change agenda that physicians will support. Developing a shared purpose implies the following key steps:

a.   Listening, demonstrating respect for different views, and developing processes aiming at helping stakeholders shape the vision's implementation.
b.   Discussing with physicians about reorganizing care ought to focus straight on the stakes relevant for patients. As we have seen in Chapter 6, having an effective data strategy and understanding how to use and share data can be very helpful to show how proposed changes can improve efficiency and patient outcomes.
c.   Promoting your statement of purpose and putting its principles into action. An array of communication tools can be used to reinforce an organization's message of shared purpose such as internal training videos, newsletters, and storytelling.

3. Self-Interest

Physicians' self-interest in financial incentives and job security can be channeled to reinforce engagement in a number of ways such as:

a.   Making portions of physicians' compensation dependent upon performance.
b.   Putting physicians on straight salary.

Either approach, when used to advance goals that are consistent with shared purpose, can have sustained effectiveness. Indeed, if physicians are confident that a particular management-endorsed behavior or practice will improve patient care, even minimal financial incentives will be enough to help them implement it consistently. If they are uncertain about whether it will actually improve care, even large incentives will produce only marginal success.

4. Respect

Physicians value positive opinion, and tend to be concerned about losing their colleagues' admiration and esteem. Most leading organizations are more and more introducing physician performance evaluations which may include reporting how their personal performance compares with their colleagues' in ways that intensify peer pressure. Such scrutiny can be excruciating, especially when the data are "unmasked" so that colleagues can see one another's results

Most healthcare organizations already use one or more of the four motivational levers described here. Indeed, the most successful rely on all four.

5. Tradition

Having a strong sense of belonging to an organization highly contributes to motivate physicians to adhere to that organization's standards and traditions. For example, doctors have followed the Mayo Clinic's dress code since the clinic was founded, in the late nineteenth century. The requirements today include neckties for men and hosiery for women, even in Mayo's facilities in Arizona, where temperatures routinely top 100°F.

Thus, in order to make sure that you deliver the message in a positive way which is relevant and appealing to physicians, it is critical to choose the messages and messengers very carefully.

Make physician involvement very noticeable because, given their camaraderie with other physicians, when they are placed in leadership positions, others will notice and start to trust the administration supports them because colleagues they admire and appreciate have a role in the process.

Let physicians feel ownership even when dealing with issues apparently out of their scope such as supply chain management.

Communicate early, honestly and frequently. Value physicians' time as their culture and workflow is quite different from other stakeholders in the hospital: attending a meeting requires a physician to take his/her time either before or during clinic hours, with a consequent impact on their ability to meet and take care Of his/her patients.

Physician engagement requires leadership and trust

People, including physicians, resist loss (or possible or perceived loss), not the change itself. Thus it is important to keep the patient as the "North Star" with the end goal being the delivery of better care for patients.

Physicians will buy into a new methodology much more quickly if they are engaged in its development and are treated as partners with the hospital or healthcare organization. Thus, make sure to engage them early. Ask them how patient care can be improved. Because the underlying supposition is that improving patient care will allow for fewer mistakes, reduce waste and provide patients the right care at the right time in the right place.

Working with the real leaders and early adopters and the early majority will come and follow. Don't waste time on the laggards because they may never get on board. Spending more time and energy engaging the leaders and early adopters will move the entire curve.

As highlighted in Chapter 7, it is key to identify real leaders and early adopters, those who drive change from within the hospitals, clinics and the organization, and equip them with the right tools, the right education, and the right resources.

If your project is large, choose one area of focus. One of the toughest aspects of a large project is getting it started. The scope is so intimidating that you can easily find yourself doing nothing. Since people have short memories, any early enthusiasm you were able to generate will quickly dissipate if no progress is being demonstrated. To avoid that very real concern it's best to choose one small area to start—preferably one where there is low risk and high reward.

Once you've selected your starting point, organize your guidance team. Based on my experience, the most critical aspect is to include someone from each area that interacts with the patient.

You are not getting too far without creating a support structure and aligning resources within the organization to provide the infrastructure for change. Without this, it is really difficult to implement and sustain change.

It is critical to understand and mitigate real and perceived loss as long as you realize that it might take a lot of discussion and a lot of consideration. There is no magic formula or standard solution that can be implemented throughout the entire organization. It must be addressed at the local level.

Most importantly, once you have a plan, follow it. It is too easy to get caught in the weeds, especially with a project that has many moving parts. When that happens, the project can stall and the people you need most can lose faith. Establishing a solid plan, and then fanatically sticking to it, will help you avoid those pitfalls and maintain the enthusiasm you'll need to see the project completed and, more importantly, embraced by the organization.

Clinicians are scientists by training, and they like to see measureable evidence of success. The more you can present data to show how the methodology you're using has driven improvements in overall performance, reductions in error or improved finances, the more they will support the change you're trying to make. Once you have the numbers, be sure to communicate your successes as widely as possible across the organization. Use the credibility of your leaders/ evangelists to spread the word. You don't want to be an underground success— you want to share your data with everyone who needs to know.

Finally, create trust. Whatever is the promise you made, it must be delivered upon. Building trust is the most important piece of the process. Communicate often and candidly. Address concerns and issues in a timely and obvious manner. Identify and overcome barriers to engagement. The administration and leadership within the organization must be very responsive.

Finally, remember to use each success as a building block to drive long-term, sustainable change in the future.

> "Physician empowerment requires management's commitment to develop and implement an empowering internal environment."

Notes

1 Tait D. Shanafelt et al. (2017), "Executive leadership and physician well-being." *Mayo Clinic Proceedings*, 92(1), 129– 146. [online]. Available at www.mayoclinicproceedings. org/article/S0025-6196(16)30625-5/fulltext [Accessed March 23, 2018].
2 Ilene MacDonald (2016), "Mayo Clinic: 9 ways to engage physicians, prevent burnout." [online]. Available at https://www.fiercehealthcare.com/healthcare/mayo-clinic-9 -strategies-to-boost-physician-engagement-prevent-burnout [Accessed March 23, 2018].
3 Rachael Zimlich (2015), "Physician engagement tips for healthcare systems." Managed Healthcare Executive. [online]. Available at http://managedhealthcareexecutive .modernmedicine.com/managed-healthcare-executive/news/physician-engagement -tips-healthcare-systems?page=full [Accessed March 23, 2018].
4 Dr. Bryan Oshiro (2017), "The best way hospitals can engage physicians, nurses, and staff." Healthcatalyst. [online]. Available at https://www.healthcatalyst.com/the-best-way-hospitals-engage-physicians-nurses-and-staff [Accessed March 23, 2018].
5 Thomas H. Lee and Toby Cosgrove (2014), "Engaging doctors in the health care revolution." *Harvard Business Review*, June.

Index

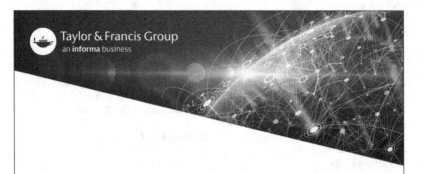

Printed in the United States
by Baker & Taylor Publisher Services